WE
NEVER
DIE

ALSO BY MATT FRASER

When Heaven Calls

WE NEVER DIE

Secrets of the Afterlife

Matt Fraser

GALLERY BOOKS

New York London Toronto   Sydney New Delhi

G

Gallery Books
An Imprint of Simon & Schuster, Inc.
1230 Avenue of the Americas
New York, NY 10020

First Gallery Books trade paperback edition August 2023

GALLERY BOOKS and colophon are registered trademarks of
Simon & Schuster, Inc.

For information about special discounts for bulk purchases,
please contact Simon & Schuster Special Sales at 1-866-506-1949
or business@simonandschuster.com.

The Simon & Schuster Speakers Bureau can bring authors to your live event. For
more information or to book an event, contact the Simon & Schuster Speakers Bureau
at 1-866-248-3049 or visit our website at www.simonspeakers.com.

Interior design by Jaime Putorti

Printed and bound by CPI Group (UK) Ltd, Croydon CR0 4YY

10 9 8 7 6 5 4 3 2 1

The Library of Congress has cataloged the hardcover edition as follows:

Names: Fraser, Matt, author.
Title: We never die : secrets of the afterlife / Matt Fraser.
Description: First Gallery Books hardcover edition. | New York : Gallery Books, 2022.
Identifiers: LCCN 2021057244 (print) | LCCN 2021057245 (ebook) |
ISBN 9781668001097 (hardcover) | ISBN 9781668001103 (trade paperback) |
ISBN 9781668001110 (ebook)
Subjects: LCSH: Future life. | Spiritualism.
Classification: LCC BF1311.F8 F73 2022 (print) | LCC BF1311.F8 (ebook) |
DDC 133.901/3—dc23/eng/20220325
LC record available at https://lccn.loc.gov/2021057244
LC ebook record available at https://lccn.loc.gov/2021057245

ISBN 978-1-6680-0109-7
ISBN 978-1-6680-0110-3 (pbk)
ISBN 978-1-6680-0111-0 (ebook)

• CONTENTS •

This book is dedicated to all those
grieving the loss of a loved one.
I hope that what you read helps
you to feel closer to those you love in spirit.

by Alexa Fraser

What happens when you die? The answer to that question was something that was unfathomable to me about six years ago, and the question was not something I longed to even have the answer to. A single thought of death made my head spin and my stomach turn; I couldn't watch movies, read books, or join in conversations about the subject.

Death wasn't exactly something that was often discussed in my family, either . . . my cousins and I were not even allowed to go to my grammy's funeral; we stayed behind with a babysitter. All I can remember from the experiences of that day was being at my other grandparents' house, getting ready to go out trick-or-treating in my costume on Halloween, when my dad slowly walked up the stairs after getting off the phone with my mom and quietly stated, "She passed." I remember looking into space, a sick feeling in the pit of my stomach. I didn't cry; I don't think I even said anything. I definitely was sad, but more shocked that she was simply not here with us on earth anymore. I remember coming home with my bag full of candy that same Halloween night to all my aunts and uncles gathered around in my grammy's dimly lit living room going through what seemed like hundreds of photos. I watched everyone cry, hearing a giggle here and there as they reminisced about the past, sharing memories of Grammy being with us. I did not like the feeling of that night. It was so dark and quiet and sad. I could not have been more confused. I wasn't sure if I was supposed to cry or laugh or say anything to anyone.

As if my grammy's passing was not enough of an introduction to death at such a young age, my parents loved watching true crime TV shows, which they always had playing in the background on television. Of course, *they* may have taken their eyes off the screen to read, cook dinner, or do some work on the computer, unfazed by what was on the TV screen, but my young eyes were glued to it. I was shocked to see all the terrible and gruesome ways people died. Of course, they were scripted TV shows and actor portrayals, but it did not help my discomfort around death.

For the next fifteen years or so, death was something I wanted to keep as far away from me as possible. This was unrealistic, of course, and in high school, I had another terrible encounter with death. One of my friends was riding his bike late one night and got hit by a car. I remember being in my first period Spanish class the next day when my principal calmly made the announcement that a fellow classmate had died. My heart and stomach dropped; I got light-headed and had to sit down at my desk. I could not believe what I was hearing. His funeral was very tragic; his fourteen-year-old girlfriend started screaming at his casket . . . you get the point. So whenever someone mentioned the word *death*, it would send chills up my spine. You are probably wondering, *How did a girl, with her biggest fear being death, wind up in a relationship with someone who can see and hear the dead?* I still wonder that every day, but I guess that is what fate is, right?

When I met Matt, I still had all those same thoughts I previously told you about, however, I pushed thoughts of dying and death down so deep that I couldn't even understand what Matt actually did. I remember sitting there with Matt at the counter-high table in the coffee shop we first met in, my feet dangling from the tall stool, asking him silly questions. "So . . . you can just see dead people walking around all the time?" He was very sweet and gentle and was probably trying to hold in a laugh or two. I think he could see I couldn't quite grasp that he was a psychic medium. After all, I was eighteen at the time; what would I have ever needed a psychic medium for? Since I would never speak or think about death, I had never even *heard* of a psychic medium before. "So, are you seeing anyone around me?" I asked him, smiling and nervously giggling as if it were a joke. I didn't expect him to say anything at all. I didn't know if he was going to start pulling cards out or doing a magic spell or weird things with his hands. He simply said, "Yes, I see your grammy behind you." I could only imagine the look on my face; my jaw completely dropped as I stared at him. I assume I was as pale as a ghost (pun intended). My face got really hot, and my skin broke out in a cold sweat that started at my head and flowed through my body to my toes. "She is right behind you." I could have thrown up. Not because I wasn't excited to hear that my grammy, whom I missed so much, was standing right with me, but that this guy I just met, who seemed like an average guy, could physically *see* her clearly behind me. My mind could not grasp what was going on. "What I'm also seeing is that you have a small bag of hers that you and your family keep and pass around to one another." Okay, that should have been my cue to run right out of the restaurant. Did I mention I also have anxiety? This was not exactly the ideal mix for me.

I tried to play it as cool, calm, and collected as possible. I jumped off the high stool I was sitting on and grabbed my pocketbook off the table next to us. I unzipped my wallet and took out a small light-blue pouch with a cross on it. This small pouch was my grammy's, and inside it had her rings and jewelry, rosary beads, and a single silver medal that my family and I pass around when someone really needs it. For example, going for a big test, a job interview, or even suffering from anxiety. Nobody outside our family knows about this pouch; how could they? I was beyond shocked, to say the least.

You are going to think I am crazy, but even after hearing the nice conversation about my grammy, and Matt reading me when we first met, I still felt uneasy with death. As Matt and I started dating and growing closer, he would invite me to his live group readings. I said to myself, *People actually come to these things voluntarily?* I would sit in the room with hundreds of sad and nervous people, trying to blend in. Matt would randomly select someone and start giving them messages from their deceased relatives and loved ones, spewing fact after fact about their entire life. People would sob, yell, and sometimes even have to sit down. The energy in the room was unlike anything I have ever felt before in my life. It was such a roller coaster that I wasn't sure I wanted any part of it. I would sit there looking down, trying to distract myself by picking my nails or looking at my phone. That would only work for a couple minutes, because I could not stop listening to the messages that Matt was delivering to these strangers, people he had never come into contact with before that moment. The feeling in the room was indescribable; it was like you could feel the closure and relief so many felt after Matt spoke to them. Those events changed me forever.

Of course, being Matt's wife, I might be just a little biased, but what he has is a God-given gift. The way he speaks to people, and how they immediately respond to him, the emotions they feel as he speaks about their loved ones they miss so much, is an incredible experience and an honor to witness. What changed me the most is not *what* Matt says (although he is unbelievably accurate, and it is astonishing what he knows about complete strangers), but *how* he says it. Matt makes you feel like family as soon as he speaks to you. He looks at you with his beautiful, kind smile and his soft brown eyes, and he makes you feel safe and comfortable. He has such an inviting and warm side to him, yet he is so electric and personable. He is truly the only one who could ever make death seem so light and special. The way Matt explains himself and what he's hearing as he's cracking jokes and hugging you can take the biggest weight off your shoulders. He makes you feel like your deceased loved one really is sitting or standing right there next to you (and they are), but it is such an inexplicable feeling, and he is the only one who can do it.

Being with Matt for close to six years now, I have completely changed my mind about death, and I've also learned so much because Matt is such an amazing teacher. He's had gentle conversations with me about the other side, educating me about how beautiful death can be, and how close the connection is that we have to our loved ones even though they are not physically here with us. I find myself asking Matt questions about death and heaven on a daily basis—while we're driving in the car, cooking together, or in bed talking until two a.m. when we should be sleeping. He has completely opened my eyes to a whole other world, and I have to say, I'm disheartened that I was closed off to it for so long. After being with him while he has performed in hotel ballrooms, and now theaters and civic centers, I have grown to enjoy and look forward to hearing every person's story and message. How Matt can give immediate laughter, happiness, and closure to someone who has clearly struggled with grief so badly after losing their loved one is something you have to see to understand. I enjoy watching and feeling the emotions of his readings, as he holds the hands of those who are struggling every day. I love being a part of Matt's courses and classes where I learn more every time I listen to him. (No, I still can't get enough of seeing him even though we see each other every day), but I genuinely look forward to what Matt can tell me about heaven and the afterlife, and what our loved ones are doing. Matt has completely opened my mind and spirit to embracing death and the circle of life, and how beautiful the cycle is. I never truly felt how close our loved ones are to us, even though they may seem so far away. I have gained such a strong intuition now, and I have been able to feel and connect with Spirit in such a different way. Matt has helped me with my energy, and he encourages me to pray constantly, to talk to my loved ones who've passed over. It has been such a beautiful journey that I cannot believe I would not have experienced it if I hadn't met Matt . . . but like I said, fate, right?

If you are anything like me, very inquisitive (and anxious at times), then you probably have many questions too! Matt's book is going to help you find yourself and open up your spirituality in ways you didn't know were possible. I encourage you to be as open-minded as possible while reading, and think about how beautiful death can really be . . . yes, as crazy as it sounds, especially coming from me!

I KNOW WHY YOU'RE HERE!

The death of a loved one is the most challenging and emotional thing anyone can go through. But the secret is, your loved one isn't really gone. As a medium, I help connect the living with friends and family members who have passed. I prove to them that the person they have been missing so badly is not really dead—they're just different. And realizing that can be life changing.

If there were one thing I could do for the world, it would be to let everyone experience life as a psychic medium for just one day. It would help remove some of the mystery and fear of death if people could see what I see. Wherever I go, I see the dead alongside the living—a daughter in spirit standing with her mother at the supermarket checkout line; a father who passed years earlier watching over his son as he takes the subway to work; a loyal pet who had crossed over, still following his owner around. Those souls are connected to their loved ones for eternity. Despite what you might have seen on television and the movies, I can tell you this—the dead are not so scary!

So often we think about what we would say to our loved ones in heaven, but have you ever imagined what your loved ones would say to you? As you make the adjustment to life without them, have you wondered how they are adjusting to life on the other side? I want to help you understand what happens from the point of view of the departed, because the more you understand about the afterlife, the closer you feel to those in spirit.

That's exactly why I wanted to write this book.

As a psychic medium, I communicate with the dead every day. But it wasn't always that way. There was a time when I pushed my gift away in a desperate attempt to be "normal." I didn't see, hear, or sense the dead for many years. It wasn't until I was in my late teens and visited a medium myself that I realized I had made a terrible mistake. From then on, I dedicated my life to fine-tuning my gift and learning as much about the spirit world as I possibly could. As I rediscovered my mediumship abilities, I became aware that everyone has a connection to heaven and can sense and feel their loved ones in their own unique way. One more thing that most people find comforting—as much as we are trying to connect with our loved ones, they are trying to connect with us. And they let us know they're with us in many different ways.

So here it is! My book about the afterlife. Everything I've written here, I've learned from my many conversations with souls on the other side. These insights are all based on my own true experiences and the messages I've received. Please keep in mind that we all have our own personal belief system. If something you read here doesn't resonate with you, take only what speaks to your heart and leave the rest behind.

Whether you're here because you are a psychic medium looking to better understand your gift, mourning the loss of a loved one, or curious to learn more about the afterlife, you've come to the right place.

I hope this helps you on your own spiritual journey!

Stay blessed and inspired,

Matt

WE
NEVER
DIE

CHAPTER 1

Psychic Ability 101

"There's a little bit of psychic ability in all of us!"

WHAT IS PSYCHIC ABILITY?

Have you ever just *known* something about another person, or pre-dicted an event before it happened? If so, you might have asked your-self, *How can I tell if what I'm sensing is based on a psychic insight, something that I experienced in the past, or wishful thinking?*

People ask me that question all the time.

The answer is, it might be more than one of those things coming together.

The Sixth Sense

Think of any experience you have. You usually engage more than one sense. When you eat a sandwich, you taste it. But you also see it, feel it, and smell it—if the bread is toasted, you can even hear yourself biting into it.

The first five senses are seeing, hearing, tasting, feeling, and smelling—but psychic ability goes beyond that. It's the sixth sense, and it allows you to see and interpret the unseen. Your sixth sense uses your first five abilities and then takes them a step further to go beyond.

Psychic ability taps into the universal energy. When you ask the universe a question, it's kind of like doing a Google search—but instead of the internet, you have unlimited wisdom at your disposal.

That's how a lot of psychics and mediums describe their insights. And just like doing a search online, you have to be clear on what you're asking or you won't get the right answer. And here's another thing—you don't really know where the message came from or how it got to you. It just shows up.

Tuning In to Friends and Family

Most people with psychic abilities have certain areas where their gift is the strongest. For example, I always know when there's something going on with a family member or close friend. I'll suddenly have an urge to reach out and call them. They may live far away, and I might not even talk to them regularly, but suddenly they're on my mind—and they won't get off!

I was taking out the trash recently, when all of a sudden, a friend of mine in Florida popped into my mind, and then I thought of their dog. The dog was like their child; it meant so much to them, and I had a feeling that the dog was sick, or that it might have even passed on. I wanted to reach out, but I felt funny about calling them—what should I say? What if I had my signals crossed and the dog was fine? So instead of calling them on the phone, I decided to visit them. We made plans to meet for dinner, and a few minutes after we sat down, they broke the news to me that the dog had passed. My intuition had been right, and I was able to comfort them by letting them know that the dog was at peace.

Intuition, or psychic ability, can take many different forms—it can warn you of something that will happen to you, a loved one, or a total stranger. And it can also prepare you for really great moments in life like having a baby or meeting your soul mate.

Trust Your Gut

So, bottom line, a psychic knows things before they happen. Lots of people have psychic insights, but they don't know it. They find all kinds of other explanations for what they're sensing. Being psychic has all kinds of benefits—but to take advantage of them, you first have to trust what your intuition is telling you.

While being psychic may seem mystical or out there—it's also a very practical skill. It can help you make better decisions about everything from job offers to partners—even the route you take on a trip. So it's worth paying attention to your intuition and learning to trust it.

WHAT'S THE DIFFERENCE BETWEEN A PSYCHIC AND A MEDIUM?

One thing you need to know is that all mediums are psychics, but not all psychics are mediums.

A psychic can predict the future—they read a person's energy and they also pull energy from the universe.

Psychics use all kinds of tools and techniques to get their information—but in the end, those are just conduits to bring the message across. Tarot cards are a great example. There are really beautiful tarot card decks to be purchased, but for a real psychic, a deck of playing cards can work just as well. My grandmother made her own special deck out of regular playing cards that she marked up with little words and symbols. She used them for years and gave amazing readings with them.

In addition to cards, psychics use tea leaves and coffee grounds to trigger pictures and visions. Some psychics do a reading by holding a person's belongings or looking at a photograph.

But here's the thing. With cards or anything else a psychic uses, what matters most is the energy the psychic pulls in. Five different psychics could draw the same three cards and get totally different insights. That's because the meaning goes beyond the card. The card, the tea leaves, the photo—whatever the tool—is only the doorway the message comes through.

Picking Up Messages from Beyond

Sometimes messages come from the energy of the person getting the reading, but they can also come from souls who have passed. Which brings us back to the question: What is the difference between a psychic and a medium?

A medium connects with the departed. They tune in to people who have died and receive messages from them. A medium can sense the souls who are around you and describe that person. The medium is like a human telephone line between heaven and earth. But it's not really black and white—because a medium can also get psychic information from those who have passed on.

Instead of picking up psychic insights from the energy around the person getting the reading, a medium will get their information from someone on the other side.

Predictions from Heaven

There was a reading I did where a grandmother came through and told her granddaughter that she would have a baby boy in the next year. The woman wasn't pregnant yet, but within a year her son was born. So, was I acting as a medium to connect the woman to her deceased grandmother, or was I psychically predicting her pregnancy?

Technically, I was acting as a medium, because the prediction came from someone who had passed. How do souls in heaven know what will happen on earth? Because they are energy—they can see tomorrow more clearly than we can see yesterday. That's why they don't worry about us. They know what will happen and they can see the light at the end of the tunnel. And because the dead are not living an earthly existence, they have an elevated perspective. They can see the whole situation with love—without any personal bias or agenda. They see life through your eyes, and they are in the perfect position to only want what's best for you.

The Tools of a Medium

We talked about how psychics use tools like tea leaves and tarot cards to get their information, and mediums have their own techniques to connect with the other side.

You'll see a medium writing on a piece of paper or holding on to a photo of the departed because it helps them to keep the channel open. Other mediums might hold your hand and close their eyes, because they need to make a physical connection.

Not only do mediums use different tools, but they receive messages in different ways. They might hear voices, see visions, or pick up on thought waves.

I grew up seeing and hearing the departed. I tap into those senses when giving a reading.

You don't have to be a medium to sense Spirit—you may get a quick vision or feel the presence of Spirit nearby—but a medium can interpret the message. It's like putting together a jigsaw puzzle—all the pieces come together to tell a story. Except it's not that simple. Imagine assembling a jigsaw puzzle you bought at a garage sale. Some of the pieces are bound to be missing. A good medium is able to fill in the pieces and bring through a clear message.

Since all mediums have psychic abilities, we can pick up on energy to do a reading, but we have an extra source of information— souls on the other side. For me, those insights are especially valuable because they are so personal.

People often ask me, "How did you know that?" My response is often: "Your grandmother in spirit told me!"

CAN I TRAIN TO BECOME A PSYCHIC MEDIUM?

I can't teach people to see and hear the departed at will. That's a gift you have to be born with. But I absolutely believe there's psychic ability in all of us—and we can use that to feel closer to loved ones who have passed. With a little practice and trust, anyone can learn to tap into their intuition and receive signs and messages from the universe in their own unique way.

The strength of your intuition will vary, and the way you receive messages may be different than everyone else's. But the biggest thing that can block your psychic or mediumistic insights is being afraid to trust your intuition or instincts.

What's really cool is that, just like you're longing to feel closer with your loved ones in heaven, they are wanting to connect with you. The secret is finding a way to bridge the gap, and communicate.

Signs and Dreams

I believe we all have our unique "phone line" to communicate with heaven. Just because you're not a medium doesn't mean you can't receive messages. Souls will reach out to you in many different ways. Your dearly departed might come through to you in gut feelings, visions, dreams, or thoughts that can't be explained.

One of the most common ways that souls reach out is by sending you signs. Those signs can be anything that has meaning to you and your loved one. Birds, coins, songs on the radio, catching sight of a person who reminds you of the departed are common, but there are plenty of unusual ones too! A sign is like an inside joke—all that matters is that it makes sense to both of you.

One final thought on learning how to be a medium: the level of your ability will be determined by your natural gift, plus how you develop it. It's like singing. I've always wished I could sing. I've practiced and I've improved (a little) and I enjoy singing along to songs in my car, but I don't have natural talent. I'm not Michael Bublé! But my singing brings me enjoyment and makes me happy, and for most people, learning to recognize when their loved ones are near them in spirit brings them peace and pleasure—and that's what matters most.

ARE ALL PSYCHICS AND MEDIUMS
THE SAME?

Not at all. The way psychic and mediumistic gifts manifest themselves varies a lot! Take my family. My grandmother was a medium,
my mom is a medium, and I am a medium. We share genetics, we're
all mediums, but our gifts manifest differently.

My grandmother was primarily psychic. She would do life
readings; mapping out the past, present, and future for her clients
using her handmade tarot deck. She relied on psychic ability, but
because she was also a medium, souls would come through and give
her more information and details.

My mom is a life psychic. She predicts future occurrences such
as: who you will marry, what opportunities are coming up, things
you need to watch out for, when you need to change direction. She
reads cards, but she can also see things in the tea leaves or coffee
grounds at the bottom of your cup. It's funny, because when I see
tea leaves or coffee grounds, they mean nothing—but to my mother,
they tell a whole story. My mom's mediumship comes through when
she looks at photographs. She is able to identify and see Spirit in
photos and bring through messages.

For me, it's different because I see visions in real life. I see
shadows, figures, and silhouettes. It's not the same as the movies,
though. These are more like glimpses or impressions. It's not as clear
as you'd expect.

Find a Medium Who Speaks Your "Language"

Although psychics and mediums all receive their information in different ways, the messages are what matters. We get information from
the same place, but we take a different road to get there.

I've often said a medium is like a translator between you and the spirit realm. That's why it's important you find a psychic or medium you connect with. It's like finding a teacher who speaks your language and communicates in a way that helps you learn.

And another thing about finding the right medium. Believe it or not, most mediums have specialties. There are pet psychics and mediums who speak to pets; there are medical mediums who tap into your body to detect illness; there are psychic detectives who solve crimes. Some mediums can find and locate lost objects.

My ability has always been directly connecting with the departed to bring through messages. We all have a calling, or purpose. Mine is putting people back in contact with their loved ones—to validate that their loved one is always with them, and to demonstrate that there is another side to life.

WHAT IS A PSYCHIC VISION AND WHAT CAN YOU COMPARE IT TO?

The best way to describe a psychic vision is that you're dreaming while you're awake. Have you ever had a daydream that someone had to snap you out of? It's like your mind took you to a whole different place. That's what a psychic vision is—it's like suddenly being thrown into a dream when you're not expecting it.

Think about how in your dreams you can visit different places and have conversations and experiences that feel real. That's exactly what a psychic vision is like.

Most mediums will tell you that their visions come fast; they're flashes of information that fly by. Sometimes the words are garbled. The medium has to concentrate to make sure they're getting a clear, accurate message. You'll often see psychics and mediums close their eyes so they can focus on what's coming through.

Insights Out of the Blue

If I'm not doing a reading or hosting an event, I still get random impressions. I might be in the middle of a conversation with someone, walking down the street, or just at home watching television and, *boom!*—I get a vision. That's been happening since I was young.

My mother always made sure I took them seriously. She taught me that when Spirit comes through uninvited, it's usually because they have an important message. She felt it was my responsibility as a medium to deliver it to the right person. She would help me figure out who the message was for, and how to relay the information without freaking the recipient out.

When I feel the presence of a soul coming through, I'll ask it questions in my head. Sometimes I ask it to be clearer or give me more information. I'll try to get a name, what their message is, and who the message is for.

My family and friends can always tell when I'm having a vision. I get a glazed look in my eyes. It can be embarrassing when I'm out in public. People might think I'm staring at them when I'm actually getting a message for them. Alexa used to get so embarrassed—"You're staring at that lady!"—but she's used to my visions now, and she can see how healing it can be when I give someone a message.

CAN A MEDIUM TELL IF SOMEONE ELSE HAS A PSYCHIC GIFT?

Many people find out about their own gifts when they visit a psychic or a medium. There have been times when a soul I'm connecting with tells me that the person getting the reading can sense and see them, too.

That's how it was for me! When I saw a medium for the first time, and I had just turned eighteen, she told me I could connect with the other side. My grandmother and other spirits had come through to her and let her know they had been trying to reach me, but I was blocking them.

It totally freaked me out! Yes, I had felt the presence of spirits when I was young, but I had pushed my gift away while I was growing up. When you're in school, talking to dead people is not a good way to fit in—and I had almost forgotten that I could do it.

I originally planned to ask the medium questions about a girl I liked and my career, but I got a lot more than I bargained for. She could see that the spirit world was trying to get in touch with me, and when she told me, my life was never the same again. My reading opened the floodgates as I looked back over the years and recognized my own abilities.

A Kindred Spirit

That same year, I found myself in a similar situation while training to be an EMT. We were assigned partners, and the moment I met mine, a voice told me that she could hear and sense the spirit world too. She was one of the first people outside my family who I actually told about my gift. How crazy is it that we both found ourselves on the same life path, both wanting to help people heal? But maybe it's not such a strange coincidence—I think we may have become EMTs because we had an ability that we weren't sure what to do with.

Although she never decided to make her gift public, she continued on her path by helping people in the medical field. Her gift made her a better EMT because she could feel things beyond the physical. She was just a hair away from being a medical medium.

Now I find there are mediums who reach out to me wanting to learn more about their gifts and fine-tune their own ability. A lot of people come to me for validation; they aren't looking for a teacher or mentor, they just want validation that what's happening is nothing to be afraid of.

I will always be grateful to the medium who opened my eyes. She showed me I could use this gift in a whole new way and how I could help people. It makes me feel good when I can do the same thing for other people.

DO PSYCHICS EVER SEE BAD THINGS IN A READING?

It depends on the medium, but I think most of us want to give constructive advice, not scare the heck out of people. You tend to attract what you focus on, so I always pray to receive information that is for my client's best good, that they can use to live a better life.

For example, if the spirit world tells you that you're going to get in a car accident, how will that help you? But if the message is to slow down and drive more carefully during the rainy season, that can save your life.

When the Loss Is Still Fresh

There are times when the person getting the reading still has a lot of grief to process. It's important that the medium be tuned in to the feelings of their client. A loved one may have passed in a sudden, tragic way and they didn't get to say goodbye. There may have been a suicide, or a disagreement that was never resolved. These are often the hardest but most rewarding readings for me. By connecting the person with their loved one in spirit, a medium can help to resolve unfinished business so that the person left behind can heal.

When the Truth Hurts

Occasionally, Spirit may bring things up during a reading that are not easy to hear.

For example, a woman was looking for advice from her mom who had passed. Her marriage was in trouble, and she wanted to know if there was anything she could do to salvage the relationship. She was desperate for some hopeful news, but based on what her mother shared, I had to let her know there was nothing she could do.

Her husband had found someone else and had already made up his mind. I dreaded breaking the news to her, but it actually brought the client great relief to hear those words from her mother. Because of her culture, she thought she had failed because her marriage had fallen apart. Her mom told her that she couldn't chase after a man who didn't love her, and she gave her daughter permission to sign the divorce papers and move on. Her mom could see that this person was not her soul mate. They had no children together, and she was destined to be a mom. She listened to her mother's advice, and after her divorce was final, was able to meet her soul mate, marry, and have a family.

Keeping an Open Mind

Some people come into a reading wanting to hear one specific thing, but Spirit can surprise you. Sometimes you'll get a message that you never expected, or you'll think you're going to connect with one person, and another will come through. I've noticed that these surprises wind up being very meaningful to the recipient. Remember how I said that souls in heaven see the whole picture? That means they know who and what you *need* to hear, even if it's not what you came for. You have to trust the universe (and the medium) and be open to what comes through.

IS PSYCHIC ABILITY HEREDITARY?

Being psychic is like having red hair or being tall. If someone in your family was born psychic, other family members are likely to have the gift too, but probably not everybody.

Take my family, for example. My grandmother and mother had the gift, and I was born with it also. My sister, however, is like the forgotten child in Harry Potter and has no psychic ability at all. It was really hard on her when I started having experiences with the spirit world. She had no idea what was going on. She takes after my dad, and he couldn't be less psychic if he tried.

We like to say that as much as I inherited my mom's psychic and mediumistic abilities, my sister inherited my father's skepticism.

Not only is it common for some members to be psychically gifted and not others, sometimes the ability can skip a generation or more. Someone will be psychic and have no idea where it came from, then they'll trace their family tree and find psychic ancestors going back many generations.

Near-Death Experiences Can Unleash Spiritual Gifts

There are times when people become psychic through means other than heredity. Most often, it occurs after a near-death experience. I had a client who was involved in a car accident and nearly died. She was on a respirator, and all hope was nearly lost. Her chances of recovery were slim to none.

Right before the family was faced with the decision to take her off life support, she miraculously woke up. When she was released from the hospital and came home to recover, she started seeing strange people in the house. She didn't realize they weren't really there. Her family thought she was having hallucinations, but it turned out her brush with death had opened up a connection to the other side.

Near-death experiences have been known to give people psychic ability, and it makes sense to me. After all, they were halfway to heaven, so it's possible for them to retain that connection even after they recover.

Sometimes an event that happens at birth can cause someone to be psychic. For example, I've heard of babies who were born with the umbilical cord wrapped around their neck and grew up to have psychic abilities.

There are rare instances where psychic ability is totally random. There's no reason; no one else in the family is a psychic or a medium. For no obvious reason, someone is just born with the gift.

One last thing. There are many people who discover they are psychic at a young age and they push it away. But it never really goes away. They can always get the ability back by opening themselves up to it again.

HOW CAN YOU TELL
IF A CHILD IS PSYCHIC?

When children are very young, they're all naturally psychic. When they become aware of the world around them and can tell the difference between the physical world and the spiritual world, most of them lose the ability. The children who don't lose the connection can get really confused. They're old enough to know that what they're seeing isn't "real," and they don't understand what's happening. The whole thing can be frightening and confusing for a child.

Things That Go Bump in the Night

I have some memories of how it was for me. When I was about four, I would hear whispers around me. I'd see strangers at the foot of my bed, or dark shadows. They were so scary! I'd open my eyes and see a shadow, then suddenly there'd be the figure of a man. The whispers would get louder and louder, and I'd scream like crazy for my mom.

My mom knew what was going on, and she didn't want me to be afraid. She would stand right next to the ghosts and show me that they weren't hurting her. She reassured me that she had the same visions as a child and her mom had comforted her in the same way. She said I had to listen to the messages because they were important. She let me know that they were souls who had passed, neighbors and people who had worked nearby. She begged me to listen to them, but I still wouldn't do it. But having my mother believe me and try to help me made it a lot easier to deal with everything that was happening.

Different Children Have Different Gifts

If a child is born with gifts like mine, it's like they're living in the movie *The Sixth Sense*. But we're not all the same. Some children are born being able to predict future events, others can connect with the departed, others are super sensitive empaths who tune in so strongly to the emotions of others that it's like they are experiencing the feelings themselves.

It's important that you pay attention when your child is growing up—especially if you have other psychics or mediums in your family. Imaginary friends can actually be spirits who have passed on. It's normal for psychic children to be visited by people who have passed on before them, who they wouldn't have ever known in life. And it's not limited to young souls. The visitors can be any age.

If you feel like your child is spiritually gifted, have open conversations with them. Ask them who they are seeing, what they are seeing, what they sense about that spirit, and what they feel when they are around.

Visits from Grandpa

I had a friend whose son was seeing and hearing the departed. She was completely freaked out because he would have conversations with himself and play for hours with someone who was not there. She came to me and asked for my guidance. Right away I could see that the boy was communicating with her father, his grandfather, who had died before the child was born.

I told her to show her son a photo album and ask him to show her who he was talking to. He immediately pointed out her dad. "That's the man who comes to play with me!"

Not believing it at first, she asked her son what the visitor was like. "He's nice to me, and he's always chewing bubble gum." The woman started to cry because her father had a bubble gum habit when he was alive. After their conversation, she made sure to tell the boy stories about his grandfather so he would understand who his visitor was.

Even if they hang on to it for a while, some children will grow out of their gift. The children who hold on to the connection will remain psychic through their adulthood.

CAN PSYCHICS PREDICT THE LOTTERY?

If I had a dollar for every time I've been asked this question, I wouldn't need to win the lottery—I'd be rich! Sadly, the answer is no.

I always think of the scene in the movie *Bruce Almighty* with Jim Carrey. Jim Carrey gets to play God for a day, and in one scene he is bombarded with prayers coming from all around the world. He tries to give everyone what they're praying for, and tons of people are praying to win the lottery. He grants them their wishes, but since so many people win, it dilutes the winnings leaving no winnings at all. It's a fact—even if you have psychic ability, you can't game life.

You Can't Predict Life—and I Wouldn't Want to

As a psychic, there's a limit to the amount I want to know about what life has in store for me and my family. I don't think it's right to use my gift for that, and I wouldn't want to anyway. I think it's important to experience events as they come. We're all here on earth to go through challenges and learn life lessons, and there's no way around that.

Souls in heaven want to help us and guide us, but we can't skip steps. The universe will always give us what we need, not necessarily what we want.

So when you see a psychic or a medium and wonder how they'd do in Las Vegas, know that we're just like anyone else. My mediumship is a gift, but it's not just for me. It's my responsibility to use it to help others. Of course, it does benefit me too, because it allows me to spend my life doing something I love—helping and healing people.

GOING DEEPER
Exploring Your Spiritual Connection

Each psychic has their own unique way of connecting to the other side.

You've probably heard of clairvoyance, and maybe you even think of that word as being synonymous with psychic. Actually, clairvoyance is only one of the ways that psychics and mediums receive messages. Here are a few of the most popular *clairs* and how they feel to the medium.

CLAIRVOYANCE—SEEING: If you're psychic in this way, it means you have the ability of "clear seeing"—you see things with the mind's eye, also known as the third eye. Pay attention to your daydreams and what you think is your imagination. Share what you are seeing with others— what might not make sense to you, could make sense to a friend or family member. They can help you decode what you are seeing. Try to clear out your own thoughts to allow your psychic insights to shine through. You can do this through meditation.

CLAIRAUDIENCE—HEARING: If you're psychic in this way, you may hear Spirit talking to you. The words aren't crystal clear like a phone call; the medium usually has to piece them together. What comes through is often fast and jumbled, or it can be a mix of voices that sound like what happens when you scroll through the channels on a radio. The biggest messages come through the smallest voices, so tune in to the words that are presented to you. Try asking questions to someone who has passed, and listen for their responses.

CLAIRSENTIENCE—SENSING / FEELING: This is the ability to feel the presence of Spirit. You might feel a chill up your spine or sense you aren't alone in a room. You might even feel someone watching you. If you feel those sensations, it's okay to ask who is in the room with you and invite them to identify themselves. For example, say, "Mom, if that's you, give me a sign to let me know you're here with me."

CLAIRCOGNIZANCE—KNOWING: If you're psychic in this way, you just "know things" without any prior information. This is commonly described as a flash of understanding, a premonition, or a sudden understanding that comes out of nowhere. If you have this gift, you are very intuitive and need to trust your gut, so if you feel something, act on it. Intuition is a "psychic muscle"—the more you listen to it, the stronger it becomes.

CLAIRALIENCE—SMELLING: This is the ability to smell a fragrance being transmitted by the spirit. It can be related to the spirit who is sending the message, such as smelling cigarettes or pipe tobacco for someone who smoked or catching a whiff of the soul's favorite perfume. When you get this smell, think of the person who comes to mind. This is the easiest way to find out who is with you.

Do any of these abilities "feel" like you? Now that you're familiar with the *clairs*, pay attention to insights and hunches that you experience as you go about your life, and notice if you have seen, smelled, heard, sensed, or known that Spirit was sending you a message. Keep track of these incidents in a notebook and look for patterns!

CHAPTER 2

The Truth About Heaven

"When you die, you're invited to the biggest family reunion of all time!"

WHAT HAPPENS WHEN YOU DIE?

People ask me this question a lot, but I notice that they get nervous waiting for me to answer. I think they're a little afraid of knowing the answer. After all, most people's biggest fear is losing a loved one or dying themselves. Actually, both. Let's make this less stressful. Take out the word *death* and substitute *transition*. "What happens when you transition?"

First of all, you are not just a body. Not even close. Deep within you there is a soul, and that soul is eternal (more about that later). With that in mind, there are a few things you should know about passing on.

Easing into the Afterlife

Nobody goes to heaven kicking and screaming. When you are about to pass, angels, loved ones, and pets who are already on the other side help guide you through the transition. Some of them arrive early, and that's the reason many people appear to see loved ones and have conversations with them before they die. I know this because of my connection with souls on the other side, but people who have had a near-death experience will tell you the same thing. That's one of the reasons virtually no one comes out of an NDE (near-death experience) quite the same as they were before it happened.

When someone passes from old age or illness, loved ones visit them and prepare them for the transition. But there's not always time for that. When death is sudden, like a car accident, the transition is instant.

Many souls tell me that dying suddenly was like going to sleep—except they fell asleep on earth and woke up on the other side. It's like when you were a little kid and fell asleep in the car. Your dad would carry you into the house and you'd magically wake up in your bed. For some, it's like that—they close their eyes and open them in heaven.

Leave the Bad Stuff Behind

Souls have explained that you see a tunnel of white light when you pass. As you approach the white light, fear or resistance is replaced by a sense of calm. At that point, you're not in your human form any longer. But even though your body and possessions are left behind, your soul still carries with it your personality, memories, sense of humor, and the love in your heart. That's why a medium can help you recognize your loved one by their memories and personality. Otherwise the medium would tell you, "I have a beautiful, serene being coming through, with no pain and worries." And you'd have no idea who that was!

When your soul leaves your body, all the pain and illness is left behind. Even though your loved ones on earth feel the loss and are sad, on the other side, there is a joyful reunion with those who have passed before you. Suddenly everything that happened to you makes sense. It's not until you pass on that you can see the full meaning of your life.

WHERE IS HEAVEN?

Heaven is an invisible world made up completely of energy that is right here among us. It's nowhere and everywhere. Like electricity, it's all around us, but we can't see it. To the living it seems like a far-away place, but to our loved ones in spirit, it feels like they have never left earth. They're still connected to the earth because of the people they love and watch over.

As a medium, I feel the presence of heaven all around me. Some people think of their loved ones as in the air, the sky and the clouds, but they're closer than that.

"Okay, Matt," you're probably thinking. "That's not an answer. Can you be a little clearer about where heaven actually is?" All I can tell you is this. If you have ever had a dream of a loved one who has died, then you have had a glimpse of what heaven is like.

Heaven Has No Limits

People ask me how souls can be in many places at once. Some spiritual teachers will talk about quantum physics and explain that there's a time and space continuum, but I can't even go there! I like to keep it simple and say that it's like a conference call. People are in different places, different time zones, living and dead, but they can connect virtually. And in this case, they can be on many calls at once.

Another way to describe it is with this simple analogy. We're all under one sun, and it feels like it's right in our backyard, but actually, people all over the world can see it.

Heaven is a place made entirely of energy, and that's why it can never be seen, altered, or destroyed by the living. I'm a medium, but I'm still a physical being. My impressions and insights about heaven come from my connection to souls who reside there and not from personal experience.

WHAT DOES HEAVEN LOOK LIKE?

Heaven can be compared to something you experience in your dreams, because it can be anything you want it to be. A great dream is going to be different for everyone, and heaven is the same. You'll experience your own paradise surrounded by the things you love.

For some, heaven is a place of rolling landscapes, beautiful mountains, and flowers; to others, it's a magical city—a clean, idealized version of a city on earth.

"Design Your Own"

Your idea of heaven is going to be different than mine, because souls create their own version that makes them happy, and that's the energetic space where they reside.

I know it's hard to fathom, but I think of heaven as a big condo building. The building looks the same on the outside, but inside no two units are alike. There are varying floor plans and each unit is decorated in its own unique style. That's the reason why religion flows so harmoniously in heaven. Everyone can have a different religion and a different idea of heaven, and that's what they experience when they die—but they're all in the same "place."

And here's another crazy thing. You can be with a loved one in heaven—together—and both of you will perceive your environment differently.

A Fisherman's Dream

I did a reading for a woman whose husband was a fisherman. When I connected with him, he was on a boat in the middle of the ocean, doing what he loved most. His wife was a little freaked out because she wanted to be with him after she died, "but not in a fisherman's heaven!" I had to explain to her that she could still be with him while having her own version of heaven. The great thing about heaven is that you don't have to compromise, because everyone gets what they want.

Some people don't want anything to be different than what they had on earth. Many souls come through sitting in the same house they lived in all their lives. They loved their home, so they carried it over and made it their heaven. It's the same with clothing and jewelry. Souls come through wearing their wedding ring, even though the actual ring is here on earth. It doesn't make a difference whether the ring was sold, is sitting in a safe-deposit box, or their daughter is wearing it.

That doesn't mean that there is a jeweler in heaven. Just like we put ourselves together with clothing and accessories on earth, in heaven we reflect the things that are meaningful to us. A grandmother who loved to have her whole family to Sunday dinner might show up in an apron because that symbolizes who she was in life and what she loved. Who would Michael Jackson be without his white glove? You can be sure if he came through to a medium, he'd be wearing it.

DO PEOPLE IN HEAVEN HAVE JOBS?

Souls don't have jobs in the traditional sense, but we all have a purpose that doesn't end when we die. There are no Starbucks, Macy's, or Dunkin' Donuts in the afterlife, but souls have divine jobs that can be classified as God's work. The departed are often tasked to help us successfully navigate the same challenges they themselves struggled with in life.

I once connected with a soul who had lived and died in the grips of an addiction and had left behind friends and family members with the same problem. When he passed it became his job to watch over them. In his case, they were people he knew, but it doesn't have to be that way. He could have been tasked to help strangers, too.

The "Nudge" You Should Never Ignore

When this topic comes up, I get a lot of questions, usually along the lines of "How is that possible?" or "How do they do that?" It's hard to imagine how a soul in heaven can make a difference in our earthly lives. Well, they don't swoop down on a white horse or show up with angel wings. Instead, they will intervene in very subtle ways to nudge a person on earth in the right direction.

If someone is having suicidal thoughts, a soul might see what's happening and alert a family member. Often they will nudge them to check on that person and prevent a catastrophic event. We call this divine intervention, and it's a joint effort between a soul in heaven and someone on earth. That's why you shouldn't push aside those random urges or thoughts to reach out to someone, no matter how odd it might seem.

In some instances, divine intervention goes straight to the person in danger, providing guidance to lead them out of a crisis. The person whom they've helped might have a feeling that something otherworldly was guiding them. I've had several people come to me for readings just because they experienced something where they were mysteriously delayed and avoided an accident or other catastrophe. They know something extraordinary happened and they're either looking for confirmation, or they want to say thank you.

Coincidence or Divine Intervention?

A friend told me this story and asked if I thought it was a divine intervention. I'm pretty sure it was! She was driving around one day, running errands, and got a strong urge to touch base with a neighbor whom she hadn't spoken with in years. The two women had a small disagreement and had drifted apart. When her estranged neighbor answered the phone, she was shocked. "I can't believe you called at this exact moment!"

It turned out the woman was sitting with her mother, who had unfortunately passed away hours earlier in her apartment. The landlord had called when the bathtub the elderly woman had been sitting in overflowed into the apartment downstairs, and when she opened the door, she found her mother's body in the tub. It was a horrifying experience, and she desperately needed to hear a friendly voice while she waited for the coroner to arrive. Was it a coincidence that my friend got the urge to call her old neighbor out of the blue? Both women agreed that this call was meant to happen exactly when it did!

Souls in heaven can help us out in other ways too. They might be spiritual mentors who introduce us to people we need to meet, lead us through challenges that will make us stronger, and encourage us onto our true path.

Your loved one can help you, but it also might be their mission to help a total stranger. When someone passes, their life on earth is done, but their soul continues to evolve by helping another person avoid making the same mistakes or by inspiring them to greatness. Whichever task lies in front of your loved one, you can be sure they're also keeping an eye on you, and at the very least, sending love your way.

DOES MY LOVED ONE IN HEAVEN MISS ME?

The short answer is no, but every time I say this, people get really upset. They think because the person doesn't miss them, they didn't love them when they were alive. That's not true.

They don't miss you because they are with you! In fact, your loved one has a front row seat in your life, and as crazy as it sounds, they are actually closer to you in death than they were in this world.

Think about everything you do. Your morning drive to work? They are with you. When you're working at your desk, they're there. They are with you when you're having lunch. Even when you're going to the bathroom (but we don't like to talk about that, lol).

When a loved one passes, to the people they leave behind it feels like the ultimate distance. For the dead, it's the opposite. They feel close and connected—and not just to one person. They're connected to everyone they cared about. They are with you through the good times, the bad times, and all the times in between.

Choosing Life over Grief

The last thing your loved ones want is for you to cry over them, because they're not gone and they don't want your grief to keep you from being happy and enjoying life.

The one thing that the dead always say to me, as a medium, is that they don't want you to take time out of your life mourning them. Time and time again they ask me to relay the same message, "I'm always by your side."

Visits from Grandma

The first time I heard this message was from my own grandmother. Here's what happened.

When I was four, my grandmother passed. I didn't understand what was going on because I was so connected to her psychically that she still felt alive to me.

For a long time after she passed, my grandmother would visit me. She always came at night after my mother went to sleep.

I told my mother about the visits, and she was surprised that Grandma wasn't coming through to her, too. Before my grandmother died, my mom had begged her to come back and visit her, so she fully expected that she would. But my grandmother never did visit my mother, although she continued to come and visit me. I know Mom was hurt about this, but there was nothing I could do.

Then one day I woke up with a message from my grandmother for my mom. She said that my mother was drowning in grief and hadn't let go. That was the opposite of what Grandma wanted. "Tell your mom: You have a family to take care of; please, you have to move on and live your life."

I asked my grandmother why she wouldn't tell my mom that herself, and she said it wouldn't be good for my family. Because my mom had always relied on my grandmother for everything, Grandma was afraid she would get too caught up trying to connect with her in spirit.

I don't remember a lot about what happened when I shared this, except I do remember my mother crying. I was happy she had finally heard me and accepted the message.

That's a perfect example of why souls sometimes won't come through to a medium or make their presence known in other ways. They know when you're likely to become consumed by them, and they won't let that happen. Remember, they know what's best for you, and they want you to live your best life.

Some people who are grieving want to see me every week to maintain a connection with their loved one. Souls in heaven never want to see you going to a medium all the time. There's no point in going too often, you won't learn anything new, and it keeps you from moving on.

WILL I SEE MY PET IN HEAVEN?

Yes, pets make it to heaven, and they join up with friends and family when they do. There is a reason why your pets become like family—because your soul recognizes the soul inside them. Even though they belong to a different species, an animal's soul is not much different from yours. They feel pain, fear, loneliness, but most important of all, they are able to experience and feel love.

Furry, Feathered, and Scaley Angels on Earth

We've all seen or heard of pets doing amazing things that seem beyond what an animal is capable of. It's not that surprising! In some instances, angels and souls come into our lives in the form of a pet so they can provide help and support. They might play the role of service dog, Seeing Eye dog, best friend, companion, or protector. This doesn't apply just to dogs and cats, either. I've seen all kinds of pets that were put here to be earthly guides—rabbits, guinea pigs, horses—one time even a snake!

What's even more amazing is that in heaven, pets always appear with family members and friends. Remember, it's not just the ones that passed recently. Your childhood pet is still around.

"I'm Taking My Bird!"

Once, I was doing a reading for a woman and her brother came through. I said, "You're going to think I'm crazy, but your brother said he came to take his bird back to heaven!"

Her brother had a favorite parrot, and after he died, she took care of his bird. She had never wanted a bird as a pet, and this noisy parrot drove her absolutely crazy. She couldn't shut him up! She moved him all over the house to try to make him stop talking, and one day she woke up and it was quiet.

Horrified, she realized that the bird had passed. She felt terrible because she thought she had let her brother down. But the brother came through to let her know that he had taken the soul back to heaven.

That's not uncommon. A pet might pass unexpectedly because their owner came down to bring their soul home.

Pets can break our hearts because their lives are so much shorter than ours. The way I see it, you have two choices. Choose a giant tortoise or a macaw as a pet, or comfort yourself with the fact that your beloved pet will be with you for eternity!

DOES EVERYONE GET ALONG IN HEAVEN?

Heaven is a place where all souls are at peace together. Passing over is like going through TSA at the airport. To be allowed on the plane, you have to leave your water and take off your shoes and leave behind any sharp objects. Likewise, when you pass to heaven, you have to dump your heavy emotions like anger, fear, suspicion, and jealousy. They can't come across! If they did, heaven wouldn't be a place of peace. Part of passing into heaven is about forgiving. Forgiving the people who hurt you and letting go of the things that caused you anger and resentment.

No Custody Agreements Required

Souls on the other side are all about love! That's the reason why parents will come through together to their children, even if they were divorced long before they died.

That doesn't mean that your parents got remarried in heaven. It means their old earthly grievances are gone. When parents get divorced, there are custody arrangements, but those arrangements aren't in effect when they die. They're not needed, because your parents are united in their love for you.

Of course, when I talk about parents being there for the children they left behind, that includes any kind of parent or guardian—adopted, foster, step, mentor, grandparent—whatever!

It's almost like Facebook, because ultimately everyone is linked together. You see pictures of people you've never met who are connected to people you know. It's the same thing in heaven. The moment you pass over, you have a divine connection to everyone on the other side—great-grandparents, ancient ancestors, people you never met before—you just suddenly "know" them.

I guess you could say that heaven is kind of like *Cheers*. Everybody knows your name.

ARE MY LOVED ONES IN HEAVEN WORRIED ABOUT ME?

People come to me thinking that if their loved ones are watching over them, they must be so worried about everything that's going on! The answer to this is no. Your loved ones are in a unique position to anticipate what is going to happen in your life, long before you do. Whatever challenge you're going through—a job crisis, divorce, health scare, financial problems—they can see the light at the end of the tunnel. They know that everything will work out, one way or another. That's why we worry, and they don't.

Remember, it is like they went through a filter that removed fear, worry, judgment, and negativity on the other side—and they're left with the most positive energy, so they perceive what you're going through differently.

Sometimes we focus on the challenge at hand and we get nervous—maybe even lose hope.

But even during the hardest times, your loved one forecasts the good that can come. For example:

• When you're struggling through a painful divorce and all you can see are the pain and challenges, they look past that and see you meeting your soul mate.

- If you're having a health problem and imagining the worst, your loved one sees you healthy and vibrant.

- Maybe you've lost your job and worry about paying the bills; they see you finding a job that brings you joy.

- If it's your time, and you're afraid of dying, your loved ones know that they will be able to help you through that journey to the other side.

Souls in heaven have faced death, the ultimate fear, and see it for the natural transition that it is. That's the reason they come to us in dreams and send us signs. They want to encourage us to keep going.

Having a positive outlook is one of the many lessons I've learned from the dead, and I've shared it with my audiences over and over. Rather than waiting until you cross over, you can dump your negative emotions before you die. No one is going to try to stop you, and I promise you'll be a lot happier!

Life is how you look at it. When you approach things with fear and worry, it colors the whole experience in a negative way. If you can approach life with trust, compassion, and optimism, you'll enjoy your life so much more.

One more thing. How often do we worry about things that never happen, or if they do, they turn out to have a silver lining? From their heavenly perspective, your loved ones can see all that, and that's why they don't worry about you!

WHAT LANGUAGE DO
THEY SPEAK IN HEAVEN?

There are no spirit translators. They're not needed, because the language of spirit is universal. In heaven, everyone can understand each other, and that goes beyond human communication. Souls of humans and animals can talk to each other too.

That's why as a medium, I am able to work with clients from all over the world, and I do readings for people who didn't speak the same language in life. But don't get me wrong—I'm still a living being, and I don't communicate with souls in the same way as they communicate with each other.

Putting Together the Pieces

The way souls speak is different when they come through to a medium. When relaying a message through me, they use my whole body to communicate. I don't hear full sentences, or full conversations. It's bits and pieces, images and impressions, that I put together to form a message.

Your loved one won't come through and say, "Tell my daughter I see her new house on Blueberry Lane." They'll show me visions of that house, including what it looks like, where it is, what's around it. They'll show me the family living in the house. I'll usually get a few words, too. Based on all that, I can tell the person that her mother sees where they are living, and how she feels about it.

Souls are very ingenious about how they get a message through, but the one thing that is tough to translate are names that are not familiar to me. The souls know this and try to share things using my frame of reference. For example, if someone has an unusual or foreign name that I might not pick up, like Frangelica, they might give me a pronunciation I'm more familiar with, like Angelica. That's why sometimes names that I get are often close, but not exactly right.

For me, when Spirit speaks, it's like they whisper in my ear. Every so often, they will throw in a word from a different language that I can pass on to the person getting the reading.

A lot of times, the messages don't really mean anything to me. I don't know what the soul is referring to, but I take what I sense, feel, see, and hear and put it together in a way that tells a story that the person receiving the message can recognize.

Bridging the Language Gap

A while ago, I was on tour, doing a reading for a woman in the audience. I was delivering a detailed message from her mom. The more I shared what her mother was saying, the more the daughter looked at me in disbelief. Finally, as I was doing the reading, I asked the mother in spirit, "How come your daughter isn't validating what I'm saying?"

The mother told me that she had never spoken English when she was alive, and her daughter had a hard time accepting that I was actually communicating with her. I told the woman in the audience that her mom could see she didn't believe me because her mom hadn't spoken English. The woman in the audience thought I was reading her mind, but those few words from her mother sealed the deal! She was able to accept the messages from her mom, and everyone in the audience learned something new about the language of heaven that day.

Since the dead are likely to send the living signs rather than speaking to them directly, language isn't an issue that comes up often. So for now, look for signs and signals, and know that when you pass, you will be able to communicate in the universal language of Spirit.

And that includes talking to your old Italian great-grandma, your ancestors from Sweden, or your basset hound.

WHAT IS THE "OFFICIAL RELIGION" OF HEAVEN?

There isn't one! Heaven is not a place that's separated by religion. We all make it to the same place, regardless of faith. When you pass on, it's not like an airport with a terminal for each religion to check in. Everyone goes to heaven, even if they had no religion at all.

Heaven's "Open Gate" Policy for All Religions

I was once doing a mediumship event when I sensed a man standing behind his daughter. He was determined to get a message through to her. "Tell her that I'm here, in heaven!" He had never believed in a higher power or heaven while he was alive, and he wanted her to know that despite his lack of faith, he had made it. He told me that he and his daughter had argued before he died. She believed in heaven and the afterlife, and he wasn't having any of it! But he made her a promise: "If I'm wrong, and there is a heaven, I will find a way to let you know!" Little did any of us know that he was going to use me to deliver that message. The moment I relayed his message, she immediately got the chills. She was happy to have confirmation that there was a heaven, plus she was able to let go of the worry that because her father wasn't a believer, he wouldn't make it there.

Not only does heaven not discriminate by religion, but I've learned as a medium that no matter what religion you are, your loved ones come through the same way.

Heaven might look different for people of different religions. It will always be the right heaven for them, and just like there are different of versions of heaven existing together, different religions can coexist there as well.

I was born a Catholic and now consider myself to be more of a spiritualist. In my office I have statues of Buddha, Ganesh, Mother Mary—and each of them gives me a sense of peace. I have learned so much by studying different religions, and I believe there's something to learn from each of them. I do visit various houses of worship from time to time. There is a wonderful connection that comes from people worshiping and praying together. Many people believe that prayer is the best way to connect to heaven. I agree, but that prayer can be anything from a hymn, a poem, a Bible verse to just taking a minute to say a kind word or appreciate the wonder of nature.

GOING DEEPER
Visualizing Your "Personal Heaven"

What does heaven look like to you? If you could create your own perfect place, what would it be like?

As you learned in this chapter, we all have our own version of heaven. I know that's a little hard to understand, but let's get started by imagining what *your* heaven will look like while you're still in this world.

Here's a template that will lead you through imagining your own special place. Take your time to visualize, and let your mind wander. Have fun filling in the blanks.

Before you begin, take a few deep breaths and clear your mind. Let go of logic and try to tap into the truest part of you. Let your everyday thoughts go, and imagine yourself in a perfect place designed just for you. Look around you and ask yourself these questions:

- When you picture your perfect environment, are you inside or outside?

- What is around you? Can you see buildings, mountains, the ocean?

- What season is it? Is it snowing, raining, or sunny?

- Do you see people? Are they in the distance, or with you?

- Who are the people and what are they doing?

- Are there animals around you? Where are they, and what is your connection to them?

- What are you doing? Are you sitting quietly, or doing something like fishing or bowling?

- What are you wearing? Are you in sweats or a tuxedo?

- Is the space you are in familiar, like your own home or somewhere you have visited—or is it a spot you have imagined?

- How are you feeling? Open your mind and visualize a place where you feel positive emotions. You might feel joyful, calm, or inspired—but your own perfect space has to make you feel good!

Now that you've imagined your own idea of heaven, have a friend do the same exercise and compare notes. You'll probably find that your vision and theirs are very different—and that's the point! It's like I said earlier: just like you can live in a condo that is decorated and painted very differently from your neighbor's, in heaven, you are surrounded by others living in their own versions of heaven, as well.

Once you've decided on your own personal paradise, make some notes or draw a picture to cement the vision in your mind. You'll probably find that imagining this gives you a preview of heaven that is joyful and helps you feel closer to loved ones who have passed.

CHAPTER 3

Angels, Signs, and Spirit Visitations

"Even when you don't feel them, your loved ones are always by your side, leading you, guiding you, and watching over you."

Many people are fascinated by angels and spirit guides, and it's no wonder! Life can be challenging, and just about everyone could benefit from having a heavenly presence to watch over them and help them along. But it's rare to actually see an angel as you go through your day-to-day life. So how do you know when you're getting guidance, encouragement, and protection from a divine source?

Before we get into the details, let me start with a story. . . .

I have a good friend who is in the marketing business. He'd spent years at the same company when he started feeling it was time for a change. He loved the people at his job, and they loved him, but he was bored doing the same thing every day, and his career felt like it had stalled. He started looking into new companies and found an opportunity that appeared too good to be true. The office was walking distance from his house, the hours were perfect, and the pay was more than what he was currently making. He was so excited that he applied for the job immediately. He didn't think he would even get a call back, but within a week's time, he was called in and interviewed by the whole team.

He came home from the final interview with a job offer and a folder full of paperwork to fill out, emblazoned with the new company's unusual octopus logo.

Despite his excitement, he had a nagging feeling that he shouldn't give notice just yet. A few days passed, and he still couldn't bring himself to break the news to his boss.

One evening, he took a walk on the beach, hoping to clear his head so he could move forward with his plan. It was a beautiful night, and the sun was starting to set. In the golden light he spotted something that made him pause. It was a sign with an image that looked oddly familiar. The sign read, BEWARE OF OCTOPUS, and the octopus on the sign matched the one on the logo of his new company. He had a feeling in his gut that this was a warning he shouldn't ignore.

Worried that they'd think he was crazy, he didn't tell anyone about the sign, but he didn't give notice at his company, and didn't accept the new job. When the COVID-19 pandemic hit a month later, the company he'd turned down was hit hard, losing clients and eventually closing their doors. His current company, on the other hand, serviced clients who were busier than ever during the pandemic. The company thrived, and he wound up getting promoted. He took a picture of the BEWARE OF OCTOPUS sign and kept it on his desk as a reminder of the divine intervention that had helped him avoid a career disaster.

ARE ANGELS REAL?

Yes, angels are real. In fact, there are angels sitting by your side right now. Why are they there? Well, that depends on your needs. There are different types of angels. There are guardian angels who watch over and protect you. There are Archangels—who occupy the highest spot in the angel hierarchy. And there are angels with divine jobs who appear in your life for a specific purpose.

Your Guardian Angel—with You for Life.

You may not realize it, but you actually spent time with your guardian angel before you were born, because they're assigned to you just before you start your journey on earth.

Guardian angels are like the guidance counselors of heaven. They are divine, supreme beings that help you navigate life's biggest challenges and tragedies. They are with you when you are anxious, lonely, depressed, or when you lose hope. You may have experienced your angel as a gentle voice that tells you to keep going when life gets tough—or they may come through amid tragedy with a reassuring feeling that everything will be okay.

When you're in trouble, angels rush in. For example, people ask me what happens when someone dies alone during a terrible accident. Do they feel pain, or fear, or know what's going on? It's reassuring to know that during even the worst times, you're not alone. That's where your angel comes in. Before you have a chance to suffer, they carry you over to heaven. As you enter heaven, you spend time with your guardian angel just as you did before you were born.

A lot of people ask me if their father or grandmother is their guardian angel. Not exactly. Although they also watch over you, they play a different role as a member of your spiritual team.

Angels on Earth

Based on what I've heard from both the living and the dead, I'm convinced that angels take the form of real people when it's necessary.

Recently, a friend shared an encounter she is certain was divine intervention. Years earlier, after learning that the man she was engaged to was leaving her for another woman, she had jumped in her car and left the home they shared. Desperate and alone, she contemplated driving her car into a nearby lagoon. As she sped down the road, she saw flashing lights behind her. When she pulled over, a policeman walked over to her, but instead of asking for her license, he looked at her with compassion and asked her what was wrong. "I told him everything that had happened, and he just listened with the kindest look on his face." After a while, her desperation was replaced by a feeling of hope. "Do you have somewhere to go?" he asked gently. He followed her to the home of a friend, and when she arrived safely, he drove off. She had noticed a name on his badge, and the next day, called the police station to thank him. Oddly enough, she wasn't surprised when she discovered there was no officer with that name. She had sensed that her policeman wasn't what he appeared, and when she wasn't able to locate him, it reinforced what she already knew.

Here's an example of a different type of angel encounter. . . .

This happened in my own family. My mom had gone through a hard time and was feeling terribly low and hopeless. She had been married young and divorced shortly after. She was having trouble meeting someone new and was beginning to give up hope of ever having a family and a happy marriage. My grandmother, who was psychic, encouraged my mom to pray to her guardian angel to put the right person in her life. My mother tried but nothing was happening. Mom stopped praying even though my grandma kept pushing her.

One day my mother came home from work and went into her bedroom to change clothes. To her surprise, she saw rosary beads hanging above her bed. She thought it was another effort from my grandmother to encourage her to pray. She was tired of my grandmother pushing her, so she stood up on the bed to tear the rosary beads down. To her amazement, her hand grasped thin air. It turned out that the moon was shining through the window blinds, creating a shadow in the shape of rosary beads. When my mom realized this, her anger changed to wonder. She knew it was a sign from heaven. My grandmother gave my mother advice that she wasn't taking, so her angel tried again with the beads.

My mother's faith was restored. She started praying to her guardian angel, and soon after, she met my dad and had the family she had always wanted. To this day, she is convinced her guardian angel brought him to her.

WHO ARE MY SPIRIT GUIDES?

Your spirit guides, like your guardian angels, are assigned to you when you're born. There may be one or many who are specially qualified for the job. They train for hundreds of years to learn all about you and the life you're about to live, and start charting your destiny long before you're even born. Your spirit guides were once living people here on earth, and once they passed, they took on the divine task of guiding you.

Keeping You on the Right Track . . .
Even If It Takes a Lifetime

Their main job is making sure you stay on your life path and learn lessons along the way. There may be detours and delays, because you do have free will, but your guides will nudge you back on course. They're responsible for you meeting the people you need to meet, and guiding you toward opportunities in your life.

Your guides don't just get you started—they also do their best to keep you moving forward. Sometimes that isn't easy. Have you ever felt as if you're in the same situation again and again with relationships, finances, or family drama? You wonder, *Where is my spirit guide! Why do I keep ending up in the same mess?* Your guides can only do so much. They'll give you the opportunity, but it's up to you to learn life lessons and make changes. When you do, your guide will help you move on to the next part of your journey.

Coincidence? I Think Not . . .

Have you ever heard that nothing in life is a coincidence? It's true, especially when it involves people. All the people you meet in your life, both good and bad, cross your path for a reason. There are no chance encounters. They might teach you valuable life lessons or provide love and friendship. Others demonstrate what *not* to do. Your spirit guides are responsible for introducing you to the people who will enhance your life and help you to learn and grow.

Sometimes you'll get slightly off course, and your guides will introduce you to someone to help nudge you back. For me, this involved my career. I wanted to help people and thought that meant being an Emergency Medical Technician (EMT). At the time, I had pushed my mediumship gift away. I was working as an EMT, but my guides knew that wasn't my true direction. I was introduced to a psychic medium through a chance encounter, and it totally changed the course of my life. Suddenly what I thought was my life path, clearly wasn't. My guides showed me a new way to help people, so I could live the life I was meant to lead.

My spirit guides brought me back full circle to rediscover my gift. And the moment I started on my path as a psychic medium, I could feel heaven helping me. People talked about my readings, word traveled, and the next thing you know, I was on the news and in the media. Everything fell into place, and I knew my "lucky" breaks were really the work of my spirit guide.

You'll Know When You're Moving in the Right Direction

Looking back on this I can see that if I had stayed an EMT, it would have been a path of resistance. You always know when you're on the right path because synchronicities happen in your favor. Don't get me wrong, you still have to put in the work. But when you're on the right path, your spirit guide is right there with you, helping make things happen.

Sometimes your guides will show you things you don't want to happen in your life, and by doing so, motivate you to change.

For example, I had a friend who always dated the same type of men. Everyone could see these relationships were going nowhere, except for her. I'm sure we all have a friend like this! She finally came to me, asking why she never could end up in a meaningful relationship. I let her know that she was ignoring the signs. She was being presented with good people, courtesy of her guides, but always chose the bad apples. I told her it was time to break the pattern. I advised her to get out of her circle, spend time in new places, and follow a different pathway—but most of all, watch for signs! She promised to try, and it took almost no time before she was in a fulfilling relationship.

Your spirit guides will always show you the right direction, but you have to listen and take the steps to pursue it. Sometimes the right direction seems like it's wrong. That happens a lot with divorced couples. They marry someone and have kids with them. That person might not be their soul mate, but they will help them create their beautiful children. Your path might be complicated, but it's easier when you accept that people are in your life for a reason.

Sometimes you don't even realize how much your guides help you while it's happening. But random encounters and events suddenly make sense when you look back.

HOW DO I KNOW MY ANGELS AND LOVED ONES ARE WITH ME?

Your angels, spirit guides, and loved ones have many ways to communicate with you and let you know their presence is near. When they are around, they generate a warm feeling and unique spiritual presence.

Your *angel*'s main purpose is to bring comfort, protection, and healing. They warn before tragedy is about to strike and reassure you when things are going wrong. Their ways of communication are sometimes subtle, but they deliver important messages. For example, have you ever felt a sick feeling in the pit of your stomach and sensed that something was about to go wrong right before it happened? That was likely your guardian angel signaling you. They also can come to you with more force when it's required. Out of nowhere, you might hear a voice in your ear telling you to slow down. When you're all alone, speeding in the car, that voice is your guardian angel.

Your angels come through as a warm, calm, comforting presence. When you speak to your angels, you may feel a calming sensation pass through your body like a cosmic hug, letting you know they are near.

Your *spirit guides* are your own personal tour guides in this world. They can read the map and compass to help you navigate your life. Imagine your spirit guide as a GPS for your soul. Intuitively, they are sending you signals that steer you away from roadblocks, lead you down new roads, and help you cross bridges. You won't necessarily feel them with you as a separate presence, because they speak to you through your own thoughts and emotions. For example, if you're in a job or relationship that isn't for you, they'll make you feel uncomfortable until you make it right.

Your loved ones in heaven communicate through signs, which are their main language. Signs are like text messages or postcards from heaven to remind you they're with you. That leads us to the next question.

WHAT ARE SOME DIFFERENT TYPES OF SIGNS YOUR LOVED ONES SEND YOU?

First of all, I'm convinced that if your gut tells you something is a sign, it most likely is! You know a sign is real when it repeats itself and appears in different forms within your life, and when it triggers a memory of someone who's passed.

Here are some common ways souls in heaven reach out to you:

Unexpected Smells

Sometimes your loved ones will send you a fragrance out of the blue to let you know they are close. It might be a specific cologne your loved one wore, the smell of smoke if they were a smoker, or even the smell of their favorite flower.

Coins from Heaven

A loved one in spirit might put coins in your path to send a message. When you see a random coin or penny pick it up and check the date. You may be surprised that the date will be a meaningful number such as a birthday, anniversary, or date that was significant to you both.

Music from the Afterlife

Musical signs often appear during special times in your life like birthdays or anniversaries, and they can also comfort you when you need it most. You might randomly hear a song they used to sing to you or a song that they loved when they were here. When you hear a tune that brings a lost loved one to mind, know that it was divinely played for you to enjoy.

Orbs in Photos

Those in spirit are energy, and sometimes they will appear as orbs or other unexplained figures in photographs and videos. These signs often appear in group photos where many of the soul's loved ones are gathered together.

Night Signs

Your loved one will often repeat a sign to get your attention. Waking you up at the same time every night is a common example. If you find that you keep waking up at the same time every night or waking up at the time of their passing, take a minute to acknowledge the sign and say hi.

Dream Visitations

Dreams are the easiest way for your loved ones to reach out. When you lay your head down to sleep, your mind enters into an energy space that your loved ones can use as a conference room to come and visit. They can pass you a message during that time or just show you they are happy and pain-free.

Seeing 11:11 repeatedly

Times such as 11:11 or 12:12 are messages that normally come in a time of need or during a life change or transition when you are searching for guidance around uncertain times. If this happens to you, know that your loved one is sending you a little hello to let you know they support and love you, and you are on the right track.

Lights Flickering or Random Electrical Signs

Your loved ones are a form of energy, and sometimes their presence will make the lights flicker or turn the TV on and off. This particular sign usually happens within a few weeks of a loved one's passing away, as they are acclimating to the other side.

Dragonflies, Butterflies, and Rainbows

These are divine symbols that will show up when you least expect them and when you need to know that your loved one is with you. How do you know a butterfly is not just a butterfly? You can tell if it interacts with you in an unusual way, like circling your head or sitting on your shoulder, or if it triggers a memory of a loved one who has passed.

I could go on and on, because there are so many ways your loved ones make their presence known, but the bottom line is that a sign can be absolutely anything that is meaningful to both the sender and receiver.

HOW DO I KNOW WHEN A LOVED ONE IS SENDING ME A SIGN?

Spirit communicates in different ways with signs based on the personality of the soul involved. For example, if your grandmother loved the fragrance of Jean Naté when she was alive, when you think of her and suddenly smell Jean Naté, she is letting you know she's around. Some people think of signs as standard or cookie-cutter, but it's not all butterflies and dragonflies. The signs that souls choose are actually very specific.

They always send signs that will remind you of them. For example, I did a reading for a woman whose dad was a fisherman here in Rhode Island. He loved everything about being on the water, and when he came through to me, he said to tell her that his sign to her was anchors! Her daughter laughed, "Oh my gosh, I see anchors everywhere!" She was so happy to realize that they were signs from her dad.

Souls Send Unique Signs "Their Way"

Another woman told me her husband had been crazy about Frank Sinatra. She had played "My Way" at his funeral, and she noticed that she often heard the song playing when she was thinking of him.

Another woman came to me who had lost her son. He had been a hockey player who lived and breathed hockey. When he passed, they buried him in his hockey jersey with his number 10 on it. She told me that the number 10 seems to appear everywhere—and she always knows it's her son. She glances at the clock and sees 10:10, receipts total $10.10, she spots the number on license plates, and whenever she sees it, she feels his love around her.

Signs Trigger Memories

The sure-fire way to know who is sending you a sign is to become aware of who came to mind when you saw it. Signs recall memories. If you see a dragonfly and immediately think of your dad, you know it's him sending you that sign.

If a butterfly lands on your shoulder and you think of your daughter being surrounded by butterflies, it's her.

Of course, every coin, song, or anchor doesn't have divine meaning. Sometimes a butterfly is just a butterfly. So if you don't recall a person or a memory when you see it, it's probably not a sign.

WHAT DOES IT MEAN WHEN YOU DREAM OF A LOVED ONE WHO HAS DIED?

We've talked about all kinds of signs and signals, but dreams are actually the easiest way to connect with loved ones in spirit. The reason is that spirits are pure energy, and so are your thoughts. When you sleep at night and your body shuts down, your mind starts to file away the events of the day. That clears your mind, making it easier for your loved ones to slip in and visit you.

I'll See You in Your Dreams!

Dreams are like a conference room where you can connect with loved ones on the other side. Like a real conference room, they provide a dedicated space where Spirit can convey the most complete and detailed messages. When you see your loved ones in a dream, you're actually experiencing a spiritual encounter. In your dream state, you're able to touch, feel, and sense your loved one.

Why do they visit you in dreams? Usually they just want you to know that they made it to heaven and that they are okay. Other times they will come through with a special message. For example, in my family, whenever someone is about to conceive, a loved one will appear in a dream to announce the new arrival. I remember when I was younger, my mother had a dream of my dad's grandmother holding a baby girl. She immediately knew she was about to become pregnant, and right after, she learned she was expecting my sister.

When your Dream Feels Like a Nightmare

Sometimes dreams of a loved one are not pleasant—but don't jump to the conclusion that something is wrong, or that they have not crossed over successfully. Remember that your loved ones come through to let you know they're at peace. They have left anger, pain, and any other negative emotions behind. So if you get an angry or upsetting dream about your loved one, it's not about them. They're actually showing you there's grief and pain you need to release.

WHY DO I KEEP SMELLING MY LOVED ONE?

This is actually my favorite kind of sign. As a medium, I sense and feel your loved one the same as you do—and many times they will come through with smells.

Just like I mentioned about smelling Jean Naté. The same thing happened when I read for Dr. Paul Nassif from the television show *Botched*. The minute I walked into the room, standing there was his mother in her spirit form, and the room reeked of Jean Naté. I told him what I was seeing, and he said, "That was my mother! She loved Jean Naté."

That wasn't the first time that a scent signaled a spirit's arrival. I've had mechanics come through smelling like petroleum oil; fishermen come through smelling like the seafood market; even once a plumber smelling like . . . well, you know.

Smells are special because they are a part of your loved one's essence. Do you remember your grandmother having a special smell? Whether it's lemon candy, cinnamon, lavender, or mothballs, a smell becomes part of their spirit, and it's a sure way of knowing your loved ones are there.

THE HEAVENLY LANGUAGE OF NUMBERS

Has this happened to you? Despite how early or late you go to bed, you keep waking up at the same time every night: 3:33 a.m. or 4:14 a.m. You stare at your alarm clock thinking, *Why does this keep happening?*

You may even feel a presence with you, or a cool breeze that comes over you while you lie in your bed. It may sound a little crazy, but there is a reason why. Someone you love and miss in heaven is trying to get your attention.

As a psychic medium, I have noticed that those in spirit use different ways to try to get your attention. New spirits or souls who've recently crossed over start to reach out through spirit touchpoints, the first being numbers. It's a simple way for them to open the door and start communicating with you right away.

Are You Awake?

When a soul passes, it is normal for them to try to reach you by waking you up at odd hours of the night. They are waking you up not to scare you but to get your attention. Many times, those in spirit can't reach you during the day because your mind is preoccupied with day-to-day happenings. When you are in a quiet or calm space, a spirit knows that's the best time to try to communicate. Normally, this is while you are sleeping.

In the beginning, they will wake you up at the same time and keep doing so until they have your attention. When they feel that you're aware of their presence, they will start to find other ways to keep getting your attention, normally through signs during the day. They might continue to use numbers, which may show up on receipts, coins, signs, telephone numbers, license plates—anything! Remember, these numbers are no accident. If you encounter a number that brings a loved one to mind, recognize it as a sign that they are with you.

HOW DOES MY GUARDIAN ANGEL KEEP ME OUT OF HARM'S WAY?

Your angels use a number of ways to get your attention and steer you away from harm. Unfortunately, we don't always listen to their messages. For example, have you ever had a gut feeling not to do something, and you did it anyway?

I recently heard a story from a client who had been trying to hang a picture above her stairs. She had a friend who said she would do it for her, but she insisted on doing it herself. She dragged out her ladder and positioned it, when something told her, "Stop, you should not be doing this." She was determined to get her picture up, and she ignored the warning. That was a mistake! Just as she got to the top of the ladder, it slipped, causing her to fall. Miraculously she didn't break any bones, but she was sore and swollen the next day. She realized her guardian angel had been trying to help her in several ways. Her friend had offered to help her; she had trouble finding the tools to hang the picture; and overall, it seemed that everything was steering her away from accomplishing the task. She ignored all the signs, pushed through, and wound up falling.

Angels will give you warning signs when you're in a bad relationship, when trouble is brewing, or danger is near. Of course, you always have a choice, and it's up to you to pay attention.

Sometimes an angel will do more than warn you. As a medium, there have been times when I've heard of a situation and known that an angel intervened. For example, I've been told of terrible car accidents where everyone walked away unharmed. I've heard of Good Samaritans that were sent from heaven to save the day. I've also seen angels signal pets to alert their family of danger from fire or other hazards.

Your angel will do what they can to protect you—so don't make it hard for them. If you sense that they're trying to warn you, listen!

WHAT ABOUT WHEN THE SIGNS
LEAD ME IN THE WRONG DIRECTION?

When a sign leads you in the wrong direction, it probably wasn't a sign. You always know a sign is real when it repeats itself in varying ways, or when your intuition tells you to pay attention. If that doesn't happen, it's probably not a sign. Like I said before, sometimes a butterfly is just a butterfly.

But what if you're convinced something is a sign, but it seems to be steering you wrong?

Signs never actually lead you in the wrong direction. However, the intention might be to help you learn, or lead you to challenges that will make you stronger. Earlier we talked about how some things are part of a divine plan. Sometimes signs lead you to a person who will teach you something important. The relationship might not be right for you in the long run, but it's a critical part of your journey.

Your angels and guides might show you the opposite of what you want, just to make a point. Life isn't a straight line from beginning to end. In fact, if you look back on the signs, coincidences, and random events that have gotten you this far, it's more like a game of connect the dots. One friendship goes sour, which leads you to a new friendship, which leads you to your soul mate. When the first event happened, you wondered why. Why did the signs push you toward a certain relationship, only to have it end?

Here's the answer: Your journey is like a game of Chutes and Ladders. Some moves bring you higher, and some are setbacks, but they're all part of the plan.

Sometimes we don't know where signs are leading us, but that's okay. That's when it's important to trust the universe and your own intuition. It will all become clear when you look back on your life.

GOING DEEPER
Decoding the Signs

It's comforting to get signs from a loved one in heaven, a guardian angel, or a spirit guide. But to benefit from them, you first have to recognize them! The more aware you are, the better. It helps if you track signs over time. I suggest getting a journal or a notebook and making it your Sign Journal.

LABEL THE FIRST SECTION "SIGNS YOU KNOW OF"

In this area of your journal, write down all the different signs you have sensed. They might be classic ones like butterflies, dragonflies, or pennies, or they might be very unique and personal. Write them all down and include the person you associate with each sign. For example: cardinals come from Grandma, pennies are from Mom, and Frank Sinatra is a signal from my dad. Your angels might send you songs that help you through a tough situation or leave feathers in unexpected places. Those are the signs you know of. As you become more mindful of them, you'll find yourself noticing more and more.

SOMETIMES A FEATHER IS JUST A FEATHER

If you're not sure if something is a sign from heaven, you'll need to check in with your intuition. If you see a feather, does it bring someone immediately to mind? How does it make you feel? Are you comforted, or guided by what you see? The answer to those questions will help you determine if your sign is wishful thinking, or a message from beyond.

INVITING MORE SIGNS
AND SIGNALS INTO YOUR LIFE

If there's not already an association, or you feel like someone you're missing has been especially quiet and you don't feel them around you, try assigning them a sign. Think of someone whom you'd love to hear from. Think of their personality and the things you associate with them that would be a meaningful way for them to reach you. Maybe your grandmother played the piano, or your aunt crocheted. Hearing Beethoven or finding a snippet of yarn would be logical ways for them to reach out. Maybe you'd like to know when your angels are around, but you never feel them. Try turning on the radio and sending a "thought invitation" to your angels to reach out with a song. Then keep track! Have a section in your journal with names of the people you'd like to hear from, and "assign" them ways to signal to you.

Stay alert and watch out for the signs. Remember, this is a personal connection that is already there between you and your loved ones. You're simply being more proactive in inviting them to make their presence known.

CHAPTER 4

Crossing Over

*"Nobody ever passes alone—
your friends, family, and pets are waiting
at heaven's gate to help you transition."*

DO THE DEAD ATTEND
THEIR FUNERALS IN SPIRIT?

They often do, but not for the reasons you might think. They're not there to judge. They don't care who sent the biggest flower arrangement or how far people traveled to attend. From their new, heavenly perspective, they are only interested in seeing the impact they had on the lives they touched, and to learn how they are remembered. This fits in with what they're experiencing as a soul who has recently crossed over, because funerals happen on earth around the same time they are having their life review in heaven.

People ask if I can see the dead at their own funerals. I can, and I have to admit that it's kind of creepy. I actually see two versions of the departed—the soul in spirit, and their lifeless body in a coffin. What I'm seeing as a medium doesn't sync up with what everyone else at the funeral is seeing. The pale, embalmed body is just a shell, while the soul is the true representation of the person. As a medium, it's difficult for me to reconcile the two.

That's why I don't like going to funerals. The body in the coffin isn't the person we're paying our respects to.

One thing that I always find comforting is that the soul sees their funeral differently than we do. While the living cry and mourn, they know that they're in the best possible place.

Souls Keep Their Sense of Humor in Heaven!

Speaking of Spirit coming to the party . . . I was once doing a reading for a woman whose husband had recently died. The couple had been so happy together; they were both fun-loving people, always making jokes and playing tricks on each other. When the man got sick, the couple discussed his end of life wishes. He told his wife, "I don't care what you do with my body—bury me in a thong for all I care." All that mattered to him was getting to heaven and having the ability to reach out to her from the afterlife.

After he passed, his wife was so distraught! She couldn't imagine how she would get through the funeral, and she dreaded seeing him in a casket. But, true to form, she decided to play one more joke on him. She remembered his words and buried him in a man-thong! It was under his pants, so no one knew about it except for her and the funeral director. Every time she thought of him after he passed, she would chuckle to herself, comforted by the inside joke they shared. She looked forward to being reunited with him in heaven and sharing a laugh about it. But she didn't expect him to bring it up so soon. Just a few months later, at a live event, her husband came through.

I didn't know what to make of what I saw in his hand. "I don't know how to tell you this, but your husband is holding up a thong!"

The poor woman turned bright red. She didn't expect her husband to share the joke with a psychic medium—especially with a whole audience listening!

People who were at that event still remember that reading. Every once in a while, someone will come up to me and say, "Remember the soul with the thong?"

WHEN PEOPLE PASS TRAGICALLY, DO THEY FIND PEACE ON THE OTHER SIDE?

Absolutely yes! Heaven wouldn't be heaven if it wasn't a place of peace. Regardless of what they experienced in life, and however violent their passing, souls will find peace on the other side. In fact, when they die in an accident or other traumatic event, souls have told me they were removed from the scene and taken directly to heaven by their angels, and were spared the fear and pain of dying.

This is especially true for souls who pass in tragic ways, like murder. I'm always grateful to be able to let their loved ones know they're not reliving the crime in the afterlife. In heaven, they're freed from that. You might be surprised to know that often, they don't even follow the case to punish their murderer. Here's a story that explains why. . . .

There was a woman who spent her life desperately searching for love. Sadly, she had a knack for choosing the wrong man and was always in and out of abusive relationships. Finally, she got involved with a violent man, and he was responsible for her passing.

When she was found dead, everyone knew her boyfriend was responsible. The family tried to get him arrested and tried for murder, but they were unsuccessful. There wasn't enough evidence to convict him. Her family worried that her soul wouldn't be at peace until the person responsible for her death was behind bars. They were heartbroken and kept trying to find new evidence against the boyfriend so that her soul could rest.

The truth came out when members of her family came to me for a reading. When she came through, I was able to convince them that she was already at peace—she was with her grandma and other friends who had passed on. She had found peace and love in the afterlife; it was her family who needed closure.

Her message to them was that justice comes in different forms and doesn't necessarily involve a jail sentence. The man responsible for her death was living in exile—unemployed, abandoned by his friends, and he had become an alcoholic. He was being punished enough, and she didn't want her family pursuing his arrest any longer.

Many times, those in spirit forgive the people who caused their passing. It doesn't mean they forget about it; they just trust in a higher power. I don't believe in hell, but I know that when they pass, souls have to answer for their actions and face justice in a different way.

WHAT IF MY LOVED ONE DIDN'T BELIEVE IN HEAVEN?

It's so interesting when I do a reading and the people in spirit are surprised. I think the most amazing moment for someone who thinks that death is the end must be when they close their eyes on earth and open them up in heaven. Imagine how that must feel!

In my experience, those who were the most skeptical on earth are the most excited to come through to their families to tell them what they've learned.

I once did a reading for a family who attended an event. I came up to their row in the audience with a message from their dad.

They were so shocked and relieved, they cried! They were certain he wouldn't be let into heaven because he was such a nonbeliever. But that's not how it works. It takes some people longer to believe in heaven, but growing and understanding is part of the journey.

Near-Death Experiences Are Eye-Opening

Near-death experiences can help people to see the light! They might have been nonbelievers up to that event, but they come back with a whole new understanding of the experience after coming close to death.

It's not just skeptics who question heaven. Some people are raised without religion, or with different views of what happens after they die. It's important to realize that heaven is universal and a place we all transition into. I like to say that even if you don't believe in heaven, heaven believes in you.

Sometimes it's hard to believe in something you can't feel or touch. Some people don't even believe in love, but looking back, they realize it was there, in one form or another, all along. When you pass over and look back on your life, it can be a real eye-opener. From the heavenly perspective, you can finally see things clearly.

DO PEOPLE WHO DIE FROM SUICIDE MAKE IT TO HEAVEN?

I think this might be the most important question in this book. People ask me this question practically every day, and it breaks my heart that anyone believes those who take their own life are not allowed into heaven. The truth is that they are in heaven and at peace.

When victims of suicide come through, many tell me that they regret cutting their life short. Often during their life review, they look backward and see how they could have reached out for help or made different choices.

They also look ahead and see the road they would have traveled. Suddenly they realize the pain and challenges they were struggling with when they killed themselves could have been overcome, and they could have made something of their lives.

Regrets like this can be hard for those left behind to hear. When someone passes in this way, loved ones often wonder if they could have done more to prevent it. Hearing that the soul regrets their action can make their pain even worse.

But here's something I figured out after hearing messages like this several times. The soul is sharing their feelings for a good reason. Realizing how different life could have been if they'd stuck it out is a powerful lesson, and one they are determined to share with the living. They want to protect others from making the same mistake! It's their job to let people know that no matter how bad they might feel and how hard things get, there is still hope around the corner. Heaven has a plan if we can have the patience to let it play out.

Why People Give Up Hope, and How They Find Peace

People choose to end their lives themselves for different reasons, and they come through hoping I'll let their loved ones know why. They may have suffered with depression, bipolar disorder, schizophrenia, or another disorder that made it hard to think clearly. Some suicides are due to outside factors like crippling financial troubles, addiction, or failed relationships. Some of these issues may have resolved themselves in time, while others may have caused pain for life. The soul sees that now and they want their loved ones to know they're at peace.

Lessons to Learn about Death . . . and Life

I connected a soul with his family at an event. He had been unemployed for years and his wife had been working like crazy to support the family. Depressed and discouraged, he felt he would be worth more to his family dead than alive. He killed himself, thinking that his family would at least benefit from his life insurance. What he didn't know at the time was that his wife had canceled their life insurance policy months before. She knew why he had taken his life and was both distraught at losing him and guilty that she hadn't told him about the canceled policy. She couldn't shake her feeling that if he'd known about the canceled policy, he might not have ended his life. When he passed, people rallied around her. A friend helped her get a better-paying job, and family members collected money to help with expenses. The man looked down from heaven with regret, realizing that he could have reached out for help and still been there for his wife and kids. I believe he shared his story from heaven to give others the courage to ask for help.

I DIDN'T GET A CHANCE TO SAY GOODBYE TO MY LOVED ONE. IS IT TOO LATE?

People often ask me to relay a message to their departed loved ones. As a medium, I deliver messages from the other side, but I don't send them back. I'm just an inbox taking messages from heaven, but I can't send!

The good news is that you don't need a medium to relay your message. You can send it yourself. Your loved ones can hear you through your thoughts, feelings, and words.

You can send a message to heaven at any time, and your loved one will get the message. So don't worry if you weren't there at their final moment. It's the last thing on their mind. They are not focused on who was there when they passed over; they have a much wider perspective. Looking back, they see all the time you had together—the love and laughter you shared—and that's what matters. They don't want you to put so much weight on their last few minutes, because they definitely are not!

A Lifetime of Loving Memories

A woman came to a group reading, visibly upset about the circumstances of her mother's death. She had been her mother's best friend, and when her mom couldn't take care of herself, the daughter moved her into her house for two years. They had a wonderful time—enjoying coffee, cooking meals, and taking drives together.

The mother was diagnosed with cancer and was in the hospital. Sadly, there was nothing the doctors could do, and they were getting ready to send her back to her daughter's home so hospice could take over her care. But she never made it out of the hospital. As the daughter was preparing for her mother's arrival home, the elderly woman drew her last breath. Her daughter wasn't there to say goodbye, and she had been carrying that guilt and regret around with her ever since.

Her mother came through and said she couldn't have asked for a more wonderful daughter. She cherished all the happy moments they had shared, and she knew how much her daughter loved her. That was all that mattered. I was so happy to be able to ease her daughter's mind, and I'm sure that reading resonated with many others in the audience. The moral of this story: don't put too much weight on those last moments!

Sometimes it's the opposite. We don't spend time with a loved ones in life, and suddenly it's too late. I knew a woman who was estranged from her father and didn't know he had passed. Years later when she learned of his death, she went to his grave and poured out her heart. I know he heard her. It's never too late to make amends and find closure.

Remember that souls in heaven don't want you to spend too much time mourning their passing, they want you to be at peace— because they are! As I've said before, they want you to live life to the fullest and not let their passing get in the way of that.

MY LOVED ONE DIDN'T KNOW ME AT THE END. DO THEY REMEMBER ME NOW THAT THEY'RE IN HEAVEN?

They absolutely do. Alzheimer's disease seems to erase our memories in this world, but in the afterlife, all those memories are restored. We'll talk about the life review later in another chapter, but know that souls who lost their memories in life will be able to relive them all during that process.

The moment they transition over, the memories rush back in an instant. It's like pressing rewind on an old VCR and seeing the whole movie in a flash!

But that's not the only thing that you can hit rewind on. Many times, people who have had Alzheimer's or dementia will come through feeling much younger, as if those foggy years didn't even happen.

Sometimes a soul will admit that they actually remember too much, and they're embarrassed by what they did and said when they were ill or not themselves.

Setting the Record Straight

Once, I was doing a reading and the soul who came through had had Alzheimer's when she died. During her final days, she wasn't in her right mind, and at one point she shared a shocking revelation with her daughter. She said she'd secretly had a son whom no one knew about. Her daughter believed her and started searching for her "brother." When the mom came through during the reading, she explained that she had actually been confused and was thinking about her own brother who had passed. She was very unhappy that she had upset her daughter with her revelation, and she was grateful to be able to set the record straight through me!

Again, this is an example of looking at someone's whole life. The loved one can look down and see every side of the issue, understand everyone's intentions, and have total clarity.

I can't even tell you how many times a loved one has come through and understood why their family had to get a caretaker or put them in a home. They might have kicked up a huge fuss while they were alive, but from heaven, they understand that their family was doing what was best for them. They can now understand their family's good intent.

DOES IT MATTER IF I CREMATE OR BURY MY LOVED ONE?

There are times when I do a reading and it comes up that the departed had wished to be buried, but they were cremated instead or vice versa.

I was doing a live event and I had walked past a row, when a father stepped up and told me he was buried in the backyard. I was nervous that I'd just found out about a murder! I turned to a woman and told her, "You might think I'm crazy, but your father says you buried him in the yard."

"Yes, I visit him every day," she said. "In fact, I just moved, and I dug him up and brought him to the new house." It turns out she'd buried the urn with his ashes. He loved it, because it reflected his daughter's funny personality!

Another man came through laughing: *"You won't believe what my wife did with my ashes! She keeps them in a backpack and brings them to all the places we were planning to go together, then she brings them back home with her."*

The wife explained that "He wanted me to scatter them into the ocean, but I can't bear to let them go." She was so relieved when he said she should keep them for as long as they gave her comfort.

Bottom line, the dead know better than anyone that bodies don't matter—graves and ashes (and funerals, for that matter) are all for the comfort of the living.

IS MY LOVED ONE MAD AT ME?

There are a lot of reasons people come up with for why their loved one might be angry with them. You might think they'd be resentful about spending their last days in a home, or disappointed about how their funeral was conducted. Or they could be upset that you didn't somehow intervene and prevent their death.

No Grudges in Heaven

If you're thinking your loved one is still holding on to resentment against you, or anyone else, I promise you, the opposite is true. Take this situation, for example. . . .

I met a woman at one of my events who had not spoken to her brother after a fight she'd had with his wife. He had completely turned his back on her after the incident, and they totally lost contact. She was shocked when I told her he had a message for her, because she didn't even realize he'd died.

"I didn't lose a brother," she said, and left the event with tears in her eyes.

After the event, she did a little checking and discovered that his wife hadn't told her he'd died. She came back to me for another reading. He came right through and apologized for how he'd behaved. He realized he should have been able to see both sides of the argument between his wife and his sister, and he regretted that he had forgotten what family was.

She was so relieved! She had lived with the pain of their estrangement for years, and when she learned of his passing, it gutted her. His message freed her from her guilt and regrets. After his life review in heaven, he realized that he should never have let anything come between them. He had learned his lesson in the afterlife, and I could see that his words would have a big impact on his sister's life going forward.

Guilt can block your ability to accept the message you're meant to hear. I'll never forget this heartbreaking reading:

A woman ran a red light, causing a collision that killed her son. From that moment on, people judged her.

It wasn't enough that she had lost her son and had to live with the guilt. She also had to deal with other people gossiping and blaming her. Her husband divorced her and her in-laws disowned her. People said she wasn't paying attention to the road, that she was probably on her phone.

In reality, it was simply a tragic accident. When her son came through, I could see the whole scene clearly. She had been picking him up from school and was anxious to get home. She was rushing through an intersection and missed the light by seconds when her car was struck by a tractor trailer.

I could feel her guilt and remorse during the reading, but she had blocked out the accident and could hardly remember what happened. She was hoping the accident hadn't been her fault, but I had to tell her that she had, in fact, run a red light.

The fact that she had been responsible for her son's death was so painful that it was hard for her to accept what I was telling her. Finally, I was able to get her to listen, and I told her that her son had forgiven her. He loved her and hated seeing how much pain she was in. It took a long time to convince her that her son was watching her from heaven, and that he loved her and wanted her to let go of the guilt she was carrying.

IS THE BABY I MISCARRIED WAITING FOR ME IN HEAVEN?

The answer is yes. All souls make it to heaven, including the ones that haven't been born or those who pass at birth.

It's hard to know the reason why some souls are called back before they've had a chance to live—I don't pretend to understand it. All I can do is share some readings that were very eye-opening for the recipient, as well as everyone else in the room.

A woman came to me for a reading. She had been a twin in the womb, but her mother had a difficult pregnancy and toward the end of it she was rushed to the hospital for an emergency delivery. My client made it, but unfortunately, her twin brother did not survive the birth. The loss was devastating to the family, but at the same time they saw their daughter as a special blessing and loved her so much! In addition to the love that her family showered on her, she had always sensed an extra, comforting presence around her that she couldn't logically explain. One day she came to me for a private reading, and guess what? The soul she had felt all her life was her brother. He had been right by her side, watching over her from the moment she was born.

Mothers Will Be Reunited With ALL Their Children

Another woman I met had lost a baby girl through a miscarriage. To make matters worse, she was told by her doctor that she might not get pregnant again. Back in those days, people didn't talk about such things, and she didn't tell anyone. She and her husband were able to have another child—a daughter. And she poured all her love into that daughter because she had feared never becoming a mother. As much love as she had for her daughter, though, she still had a lingering sadness for the child who had passed in the womb. It wasn't until she was dying that she told her daughter about her sister who didn't make it. Years later, when the daughter came to me for a reading, her mom came through holding that child. She had found peace knowing that her first daughter had made it to the other side, freeing her of the worry she had carried with her throughout her life.

IS DYING SCARY?

Illness is scary, but dying shouldn't be. I'm convinced that most people's fear of death is much worse than death itself. The main thing that freaks people out about dying is that they think of it as permanent—but it's not the end. It's simply a transition, another step in our soul's journey.

People always fear what they don't understand, and of course there's a lot about what happens after you die that isn't known. That's why my events are so healing for so many people. It gives them a little peek into the afterlife, and it's not so scary. In fact, they see that not only are souls in heaven free of pain and at peace, but they're able to reach across the veil and connect with their friends and family on earth. That's why everyone gets something out of my live events (in person or online). They leave with the assurance that there is something after death, and that something is nothing to be afraid of.

HOW OLD ARE YOU IN HEAVEN?

Believe it or not, there are no birthdays in heaven. All souls are one age. I know it sounds a little strange, but think about it! If I connected with a soul in heaven who died during the Civil War, they would be over 150 years old! But it's not like that at all. Our bodies are what age, not our souls. The soul is infinite, and that's what comes through to a medium.

That's why we celebrate birthdays here on earth and not in heaven. For the living, every day is a gift, and every year is a milestone along the way. But in heaven, you have arrived at your destination, and those earthly milestones are meaningless.

That's why there's no age difference when you're reunited with your soul mate in heaven. You may have passed at eighty and your husband at fifty, but when you're reunited, you're the same age. So don't worry if your husband dies before you, you won't be a cougar in heaven!

GOING DEEPER
Wrapping Up Unfinished Business

When you are fully present and open your awareness to your loved ones, you're basically inviting them into your life. They know they can reach you and that you appreciate their help.

If you enjoy writing, why not write your loved ones letters and start journaling?

Your letters might address a burning question that has been on your mind, or they might be a quick update.

Simple little letters, like these examples below, send a signal to your loved ones letting them know that you want to start communicating with them. Here are some examples.

> *Dear Grandma, today I went to the supermarket and saw a lady who looked just like you! It made me think of the happy times we spent shopping with each other. I can't help but wonder, was that a sign from you?*

> *Dear Dad, I saw the cardinal you sent to me today. I love it when you send me these little reminders that you are there. Keep sending them. I know it is you.*

If you have unfinished business, or a question you need answered, a letter may be the perfect way to gain closure. As you write, picture the person you are writing to in your mind's eye. After you're done, sit quietly and give them a chance to come to you with their response. You can even try your hand at automatic writing, sitting with pen in hand and inviting your loved one to channel their response through you.

It doesn't have to be a lengthy process, just little "love letters" to let your loved ones know that you recognize them in your day-to-day life. You can even start a "Letter from Heaven" box to keep these messages safe. When you are missing them, you can go back and reread your own experiences.

CHAPTER 5

Memories and Milestones

"Your loved ones in heaven have a front row seat to everything you accomplish in your life."

CAN DEAD PEOPLE SEE EVERYTHING I'M DOING?

Wait! Do you really want to know the answer? If not, stop reading right now. The truth is that your loved ones can see everything you do. That's right—EVERYTHING!

But before you freak out, keep this in mind. Just because he's passed, doesn't mean your father wants to see you on the toilet any more than he did when he was alive.

Souls use their ability to see everything the same way I use the security cameras in my house. I can watch and see what's going on in every room, but I have better things to do. When I need to see something, I can watch it in real time, and I can also rewind the tape to a specific time or event.

It's the same for your loved one in heaven. They have access to everything that goes on here, but they use that ability as they need it.

They don't have to have eyeballs on you at all times, they can forward and rewind the "tape" to the important things.

Souls Are Drawn to Special Times and Everyday Events

There are certain times when your loved one is most likely to be with you. They are attracted to significant events like weddings, births, graduations, and holidays. But they also can sense when you need them or are missing them, and they'll also drop in during those times just to make sure you're okay.

Sometimes a soul just wants to touch base with you. It's not much different from the way you feel when your spouse is away on a business trip, and you Zoom or FaceTime them at the end of the day just to see their face and hear their voice.

You might be able to sense when they're around. It's common for people to feel souls and spirits occasionally. Sometimes you'll feel a touch or have a sense of someone watching. You're not being haunted, and the soul isn't trapped. You're simply feeling the soul's presence as they tune in on you.

But What About My Shower?

To get back to the shower question . . . take comfort in knowing that souls in heaven respect your boundaries, and they're not interested in invading your privacy. They're actually watching you in a whole different way than you might imagine. They're not judging you, or being nosy, they just want to keep the connection open.

If you're still creeped out, think of it from this perspective. If you were to pass away and had the ability to see your friends and family, what moments would you want to be there for?

CAN SOULS IN HEAVEN SEE THEIR CHILDREN AND GRANDCHILDREN?

Yes, absolutely, and the cool part is that the children can see them, too.

When you have a baby, friends and family gather to meet the new arrival. Your loved ones in heaven are eager to visit the new baby too, but it won't be the first time the two have met. They've had a connection with the child even before it was born, and especially enjoy seeing the new parents interact with their baby. They are drawn to the love and excitement as everyone welcomes the new family member.

Like any milestone, the birth of a child can be bittersweet when you're grieving the loss of a loved one. But I've brought through so many messages from parents, grandparents, aunts, and uncles in heaven that prove they're right there, watching with love and pride.

Being a grandparent is something most parents look forward to. I remember how I was able to provide comfort to this family who had lost their father before he could meet his new grandson.

Following in Dad's Footsteps . . .

A man and his wife attended my event, and his father came through with a healing message. Shortly after the man passed, his son learned that he and his wife were expecting their first child. When the baby was born, the parents named him after his grandfather.

When the soul came through, he talked about how happy it made him to see his son spend time with the boy, who was now five years old. He watched as they enjoyed the same activities he had shared with his son when he was alive. He saw them fishing in the same spots, even using his battered old tackle box and fishing poles.

The son was in the audience and had tears in his eyes as he realized his father had been there while the two fished, played ball, and read together. The father wanted me to tell his son and daughter-in-law how proud he was of them, and he thanked them for naming his grandson after him.

Keeping the Connection Alive

Have you ever heard your child chattering away while they played, when no one else was in the room? They might be connecting with someone on the other side. Sometimes those "imaginary friends" are actually souls coming to visit their children or grandchildren. I've known of several instances where a child was going through a photo album and pointed to a deceased family member saying, "He came to play with me yesterday!"

The spirit world appreciates when you affirm their existence by showing your children photos and telling them stories. Doing this brings that person to life in the hearts and minds of a whole new generation. My family makes it a point to introduce the younger generations to family members who have passed. My grandmother died when I was three, and although my younger sister never met our grandma, she felt as if she did because she had seen so many photos and heard so many stories about her. My sister has heard so much about our grandmother that she sometimes forgets that they never actually met!

WILL MY DAD BE WITH ME
ON MY WEDDING DAY?

He wouldn't miss it for the world. Besides the fact that they love a good party, souls in heaven are attracted to the powerful emotional charge associated with weddings.

So many brides dream of their father giving them away on their wedding day. If their dad passes before they get engaged or married, it can be devastating. But even if Dad isn't putting on his tux and physically walking his daughter down the aisle, you can be sure he's there in spirit, wiping away a happy tear.

A woman came to me so distraught. Her father had died recently, and she couldn't bear to get married without him there. She'd gotten engaged, but after her father's death, she kept pushing the wedding date out.

Her father came through, determined to get his message across. He said, *"Tell her, please don't let my death get in the way of your special day!"*

Her dad wanted his daughter to know he approved of her fiancé, and she could rest easy, knowing she had found such a good man to share her life with. He assured her that he would be with the couple at their wedding, and every day after, to watch over them and bless their union.

He closed by saying, *"I hope you'll always remember me, but please don't let me hold you back from living your life. This is your special day, and I want you to focus on yourself and your new husband."*

No Regrets from Heaven

Before I was a medium, I worked as an emergency medical technician at a hotel in Boston. There had been a big wedding, and the next morning the newly married couple headed off for their honeymoon.

Shortly after, hotel security got a call that the bride's father had been found unresponsive in his bed. The staff was heartbroken, thinking that his passing would cast a shadow over the whole event. There was nothing anyone could do to revive him, and so they helped the family contact the coroner, and brought the man's belongings down to the front desk. Because I was a medium, they felt I was the best person to log his belongings in!

Inside his bag were his wedding tuxedo, toiletries, and some other personal items. I was folding his clothes when suddenly an image flashed through my mind. The man came through and told me he had a failing heart, which everyone knew about it. His one last wish in life had been to attend his daughter's wedding, and he was so glad he had been able to hang on that long. The very next day he was in heaven, and that was okay with him! He'd gotten his wish to give his daughter away at the altar.

He asked me to write a note from him and get it to his daughter. The note said: Don't be sad that I'm gone, I have no regrets. I'm so grateful God gave me extra time so I could share your special day. Love, Dad.

"I Was There the Whole Time!"

I was doing a reading for the sweetest girl. She had been planning her wedding for over a year, and during that time her grandmother was sick and in a nursing home. The woman made sure her grandmother was included in all the planning. Even though her grandma wasn't mobile, she FaceTimed her when she was shopping for her dress. When she picked the perfect gown, she brought it to the nursing home to try it on for her grandmother.

Her grandma died right before the wedding. Afterward, the granddaughter came to see me. Her grandmother came through to say, *"Don't worry, I enjoyed your wedding more in spirit."* Because she was in a wheelchair and needed so much medical care, she had worried she would have taken attention away from the bride. She assured her granddaughter that she had been watching from heaven and loving every minute—and she thanked the girl for tucking a photo of her in her bridal bouquet. All she wanted was for her granddaughter to enjoy her day, and she had gotten her wish!

DO THE DEAD CELEBRATE
THEIR BIRTHDAYS IN HEAVEN?

Because no one ages in heaven, they don't celebrate birthdays. But they often show up for the special celebrations of their loved ones in this world. Sometimes they tell me that their loved ones do something special to remember them on their birthdays. They always appreciate that. So if you typically get sad on your loved one's birthday, consider making it a happy occasion and celebrate with their favorite foods and people they cared about. You can count on the fact that they'll be there too!

Which reminds me of a reading . . .

I recently met with a mother and daughter who wanted to connect with the father of the family. He had died a year ago, and as soon as he came through, he was persistent in telling me he had been there at the birthday celebration they had for him after he passed.

He showed me his daughter walking into a hotel ballroom with a big cake. His family had been planning a lavish fiftieth birthday surprise party for a year before he died. They couldn't get their deposit back, so they went ahead and sent out the invites and gathered to honor his memory. It turned out to be the best party ever! Friends and family laughed and cried and celebrated his life. He validated what they had already sensed—that he had been there for the whole thing. In fact, he'd even looked back to watch all the planning that had taken place.

When Heaven Gives You Lemons . . .

Speaking of birthdays, those are among the times Spirit is likely to send us signs that they are with us. I remember being invited to Alexa's grandma's for dinner. When we sat down to eat, Grandma asked me, "Matt, do you feel my mother around me? Today would have been her birthday." Alexa had never met her great-grandmother, but I could definitely feel the woman's presence at the table that night. I asked Alexa's grandmother if she had received any signs from her mother that day. She looked at me and asked, "How will I know?"

I said, "If your mother sends you a sign, you'll know!"

It turns out, Alexa's grandma would buy a cake every year on her mom's birthday. That night she pulled out a pink bakery box. Inside was a layer cake with chocolate frosting. She was surprised when she cut the first slice and saw that the cake was yellow. "Wait, I ordered a devil's food cake!" She checked the box, and sure enough, it was labeled devil's food cake with chocolate frosting. She tasted the cake and realized it was lemon. Lemon cake had been her mom's favorite. We laughed when I told her, "There's your sign!"

I love that story, because it's an example of how Spirit sends us validation that they're with us.

DO THE DEAD COME BACK TO THEIR FAVORITE PLACES?

Yes, and it's usually not an exotic vacation spot. I remember sitting on the couch in a friend's living room, when someone walked by with an oxygen tank. It took me a minute to realize it was a spirit. We figured out that it was the previous owner who had COPD. She had died in the house she had loved, and hoped that one of her grand-children would decide to move in after she passed. It didn't make sense for any of her family to keep the home, so it was put on the market and sold. The woman was still attached to the house where she had lived for so many years and would check on it occasionally. She wasn't haunting the house, she was just drawn to the place where she and her husband had raised their family, celebrated holidays, and been so happy. She wasn't angry or anything like that—this wasn't a horror movie! She actually loved seeing how the new couple had fixed the place up.

It's common for people to have an awareness of souls and spirits in different places. They might feel a draft, or notice their pets staring at something they can't see. If you get a feeling like that, it's nothing to be afraid of. The soul isn't trapped. They may just be visiting a place they had loved when they were alive.

They also like to visit the sites of special places, even if every-thing is totally different than it was when they were alive. A favor-ite field where they played baseball might be a condo complex now, or their family farm might be a shopping center. It doesn't matter a bit! The actual place they remember may be gone, but it's still real to them.

The Happiest Legacy on Earth!

I always feel Walt Disney's spirit at Disneyland in California. Even though it's a completely different place than it was when he was alive, he likes to visit and check up on things. Oh, and just to be clear, he's not checking on the daily business operations or calculat-ing ticket sales. He just watches people's faces as they enjoy the park he created. There's nothing scary about the fact that he's there; it's a positive, loving energy. To me, that's the best way to be remembered. The way Walt Disney's name and spirit lives on through his parks is a wonderful legacy.

One more thing. Many people feel bad if their loved one died without seeing a place they always dreamed of going. I know for a fact that if someone died before seeing the Grand Canyon or the Eiffel Tower, they have the chance to go there after they die. Want to help them along? Plan a trip to the place they wanted to go. Chances are they'll meet you there.

And if the dead can visit places on earth, it means they can see your new house or check out your new corner office.

I THINK OF MY LOVED ONE
AT THE ODDEST TIMES. WHY IS THAT?

Thoughts, memories, and feelings keep us connected to loved ones in spirit.

Every time they pop into your head, know they're around you at that exact moment.

The same memories you hold on to are the ones they also treasure.

Sometimes your loved one sends you memories during the most random times. You're loading the dishwasher, and suddenly think back to a family member you'd forgotten about. That's no accident. They're sending you a memory as a loving reminder of the times you shared.

It goes both ways: when you think of them, it's like ringing the doorbell in heaven. Often the memories you cherish most were from the best times in their life, before they were old or sick, and they can't resist revisiting them with you.

The Best of Times

A mom wanted to get a message from her son. When I connected with him, I could see his time on earth had been hard. The man had suffered from bipolar disorder, and his life was a roller coaster of wild mood swings, meds not taken, and disappearing for weeks at a time. He was actually homeless for a while, and had died in his thirties. But when I spoke to his mother, she looked at me with tears in her eyes and said that every time she went to sleep, she would have a memory of her son when he was a boy. She saw him as he was before the symptoms of bipolar disorder had appeared. I knew that he was coming to her in her dreams, reminding her of the best times they had shared.

I was able to tell her that he was like that in heaven—a healthy, happy boy.

Often people will wonder what happens during a reading. How do the spirits choose a memory to share? Often spirits will recall their favorite memories on earth. Even though they leave so much behind, they bring their memories to heaven. Just as your photographs are prized possessions to you, their memories are their treasures, and they carry them with them. Sometimes they will share them with loved ones, just like you'd share a Facebook memory that pops up.

WHAT'S THE BEST WAY TO HONOR MY LOVED ONE'S MEMORY?

It depends. Every soul is different, but the important thing is that they're not coming from an egotistical place. They love seeing the positive impact they had on your life and want to see you pay it forward and make a difference in the lives of others. If you do that in their name, that can bring you comfort. And they're fine with that!

The best tributes take into account the personality of the departed.

I knew a woman whose son had passed away, who founded a scholarship in his name. Every year she would give away a full scholarship to the college he had dreamed of attending. She'd choose from many applicants, but she was looking for something special as she selected the recipient. Her son had wanted to be an engineer, but he tragically passed before college. Each year, she awarded the scholarship to a candidate she felt embodied the traits and aspirations of her son.

Even though her boy couldn't complete his goals in life, she was able to honor his legacy with a scholarship fund.

You don't have to go to great lengths to honor your loved one's legacy. We tend to think of honoring someone with a statue or a scholarship fund. They don't think that way. They're happy if you can use what they taught you and pass it down to others.

An Artichoke Memorial

One soul I spoke to was thrilled with the way her special recipe had become her daughter's way of keeping her memory alive. Before she died, she showed her daughter how to make her special stuffed artichokes. Later, the daughter taught her own daughters, who taught their children. The grandma was thrilled to look down from heaven and see her prized recipe passed down through three generations. Not only that, but the family would share the same old stories that went along with preparing the recipe. It was a beautiful remembrance.

You might notice that older people get very nostalgic. It's important to them that the family cherishes family stories and memories just as they would an heirloom.

Passing the Baton

Another way to remember a loved one is to experience something they dreamed about doing but didn't have time to do. For example, if they wanted to see the Great Wall of China, you could take a trip and be confident that they would be with you.

I did a reading for a lady, and her dad came through. He was a photographer, and his profession has taken him all over the world. He always talked about writing a book about his adventures, but he died before he could write it. After he passed, his daughter was going through his journals and photographs, and she got inspired to write the book herself. She wound up getting it published as a children's book with all his photos and pictures. She would never have been moved to do this if he hadn't passed—when we pick up where they left off, they always help in spirit.

My own grandmother was a medium at a time when it wasn't accepted. She didn't have the freedom to openly share her gift. By being a medium myself, I feel that I'm honoring her memory, and I can feel her supporting and helping me every step of the way.

I feel that I've picked up the baton of mediumship that my grandmother handed me, and now I'm running with it—and I know she's cheering me on.

DOES MY LOVED ONE IN HEAVEN KNOW (OR CARE) THAT I THREW OUT THEIR THINGS?

Okay, I have to ask, did you throw them out, or donate them?

There was a woman who was a bit of a hoarder. She had tons of old furniture and artwork and would always tell her children, "This is your legacy." She thought her possessions were priceless, but when she passed on and an appraiser looked them over, he determined they had minimal value. The family got what they could for some of the furniture and dropped the rest at Goodwill.

When her daughters came to me for a reading, they were convinced she was looking at them from heaven, wondering what they had done with her things.

They didn't need to worry. As soon as the woman got to heaven, she could see her treasured possessions for what they were, just things. She realized they didn't bring the same happiness to her family that they had to her. She wanted me to tell them that she didn't care about her furniture and other items; she just wanted to be sure they could feel her love from heaven.

My Own Family Worries About This, Too!

My Italian family has a tradition of putting things aside for family members, to be distributed after they die. My grandma had a china set that she wanted given to her nephew when he got married. My mom hung on to it for twenty years, waiting for the man to marry his longtime girlfriend. She finally gave up on them ever getting married and gave it to him anyway, but his girlfriend took the china when they split up. When he finally did marry, there was no china, and my mom thought her mother would be disappointed. I got a message from my grandma, and it turns out, she didn't mind a bit. Her nephew had the opportunity to keep the china, and that was all she wanted. It didn't seem important to her from her new perspective.

At an event, a soul came through laughing because her daughter had accidentally thrown out her ashes. The girl kept moving her mom's ashes into different vases, to match her decor. When she moved to a new house, she accidentally threw out her mother! She was shocked to learn that her mom had watched the whole thing, but also relieved that her mom was still with her in spirit regardless of where her ashes happened to be. She was comforted to know her mother was fine and not haunting whatever landfill her ashes had landed in.

DO WE GET TO DO IT ALL OVER AGAIN?

As a medium, I don't hear too much about reincarnation and here's why. The souls I talk to are in heaven. They have teachings and memories and lessons to share. They haven't come through to tell me they're reincarnated, but that's no surprise. They are somewhere else. But from what I understand from the spirits that do come through—reincarnation is rare.

I don't understand reincarnation. For me personally, I only want to live once. But there are some souls who need to repeat their time on earth in a new form, and when they do, they restart their own life.

The way I understand it is that reincarnation happens when there is something in our life that was cut off prematurely, so the mission and meaning of our life was never carried out. We're placed here on this world with a road map, or what many people call a destiny. That might be to grow up, meet our soul mate, and contribute to life and society in some way. Everyone's destiny is different.

If there is a soul who made a mess of their life and strayed far from their path, they may not have gotten the chance to do the work they were born to do. In rare cases they might opt to do it again and try to fulfill their original destiny.

I understand from Spirit that this can happen to children who die in the womb or shortly after birth.

I once did a reading for a woman who got pregnant many times but never delivered a baby. In fact, she had never had a viable pregnancy. She would have tubular pregnancies, and the same soul kept trying to re-enter. That doesn't happen all the time. Many babies wait for their mothers, fathers, and siblings to join them in heaven. The soul will pass to heaven and not reincarnate.

You might think that many children are reincarnated, but that's not been proven to me one way or another through my contact with the spirit world.

Many religions believe different things, and I'm not the one to confirm or deny. I just know what I've learned from souls who have come through to me.

WHAT DOES A SOUL LOOK LIKE?

The soul is the perfect version of the departed. Your soul is you, without a single flaw and without any illness. I imagine mine as ten pounds lighter than I am now, with no gray hair.

How does that work? If you're like me, there are certain places in your home where the lighting is perfect and you always look great. Then there are places (Zoom calls come to mind) where the lighting and the angle is so unflattering that you try to avoid looking at yourself at all. You're still the same person, but you appear different. You'll be happy to know that your soul always reflects your best, like your favorite mirror at home.

I've done readings with spirits who have lost limbs, and when they come through, they are perfectly whole, just as they were before the injury. And it's not just physical ailments. Mental illness, depression, sadness—all kinds of things get filtered out when a soul passes over.

How Old Would You Be If You Didn't Know How Old You Were?

Think about it! That's how old your soul is.

Do you ever look at pictures of yourself from ten or twenty years ago, and think, *Now that's the real me*? Some people never change their social media pictures because in their mind, that's how they look and feel. I have a friend who dreads the day that the DMV makes her retake her driver's license photo, because she loves the ten-year-old one!

Honestly, the soul doesn't have much to do with physical appearance. It reflects your true, pure essence. If you've ever seen a loved one in a dream, you know what a spirit looks like. They appear in your dreams looking like their true, idealized self.

I understand that the idea of a soul appearing in physical form might be hard to get your head around. Remember, a soul is pure energy and is a reflection of who they were in life, and the impact they had on others.

I once did a reading for a woman whose identical twin sister passed at birth. We talked a little before the reading, and she said the closeness they shared in the womb never really went away. Her sister was always there, hovering just outside her consciousness. She would look in the mirror and suddenly wonder how her twin would look if she were alive. She wondered how her twin would dress, and how she'd wear her hair. She was really curious how old her sister would appear when she came through. Would she be a newborn baby? During the reading, the twin came through exactly the same age as her sister. She is ageless in heaven, but I saw her as a reflection of her twin.

GOING DEEPER
Creating a Recipe Box of Memories

When my grandmother passed, my mother kept her recipe box with all her recipes handwritten on index cards. It was precious to my mom because every time she made one of Grandma's dishes, she would see the notes in her handwriting (along with splashes of olive oil and tomato sauce). She told me it made her feel like her mom was right there with her while she was cooking.

My grandmother was Italian, so naturally there were many treasured recipes on those cards! But not everyone is a cook. And with so many recipes and videos online, more and more people don't even use recipe boxes or even cookbooks.

This got me thinking about taking the recipe box one step further to create a repository of memories. Find a box that represents the person. It might be Mom's old jewelry box, or a cigar box that belonged to your grandfather. Include a photo of the departed and a few items that represent them. Make sure you have a few letters or notes in their handwriting. Now add memories! Write down some good times you had together. If you're not a writer, make notes on the backs of photos. Let everyone contribute.

When you're missing your loved one, or just want to feel their presence, you can go through the box. You can share your box with other family members and take it out during celebrations. Be sure to keep the box "alive" by adding more memories, photos, and other items as they present themselves to you.

I promise you that your memory repository will be something you treasure. and it will help draw your loved one in heaven closer every time you open it!

CHAPTER 6

Ask the Medium

*"Mediums speak a language both
the living and the dead understand."*

CAN A MEDIUM GIVE ME A READING IF WE'RE NOT IN THE SAME ROOM?

Yes, absolutely. People ask me this question all the time and are usually surprised to learn that, in fact, many of my best readings take place over the phone or on FaceTime. Think of it this way, if I can receive messages from souls on the other side, I can easily connect with a living person anywhere on earth. I'm happy to work with clients on video, but lately I'm finding that people prefer phone readings. Like me, they've learned that whatever provides the least distraction is best for the medium and the person receiving the reading.

I also find that I can pick up amazing details on the radio. Radio callers are the same as any phone reading. I get the purest connection when I can't see the facial expressions and reactions of the person receiving the message. It's the same reason I discourage people from giving me long answers and filling in information during a reading. It's best to let Spirit do the communicating!

I'll tell you this—if a medium insists upon seeing you in person or on video during a reading, that should be a red flag. It can mean they're depending on visual clues from you to construct their message.

One more thing. I like to do a reading for a single person at a time, because there's a better chance the soul you want will come through if you're alone. I stress this every time I schedule a private reading, but there are some people who don't get it, and they have to break the rules.

This Isn't a Party Line!

I was doing a reading for a woman, and her husband kept coming through. Or at least that's what I thought! I said, "Your husband has a message for you."

"No, no, no!" She swore her husband wasn't dead. I was confused, because this soul was insistent. I tuned in to get more details, and I picked up on the name Henry.

"Were you ever married to a man named Henry?"

Uh-oh. The woman got very quiet. She sheepishly admitted, "That's my friend's husband; she's listening in on another line." Well, the friend got a great reading, and the woman who paid for it missed out.

It's not always the client's fault if the wires get crossed. Sometimes a soul knows it's not their turn, but they don't care.

Speaking Out of Turn

I remember one time I was doing a radio show. The host asked if I was picking up on anything. A father came through who had died in a horrific car accident. I was getting a lot of details, but none of them were hitting home with the host. Suddenly, the producer broke in on the conversation. This never happens on a radio show, but she couldn't help herself, because the soul coming through was her father. The host was a little put out! "This is my show, and I was supposed to get the reading." But the spirit really needed to come through for the producer, because he had unfinished business to clear up with her. He'd died suddenly and never had a chance to say goodbye. After that, I also had a message for the host, but it turned out it wasn't the person she wanted to hear from. It just wasn't her day!

People think being in front of a medium is important, but it doesn't matter at all. In fact, the exact opposite is true. But there are things that are important to know if you want an accurate reading, and I'll be talking about them in a minute.

I DIDN'T GET A GOOD READING. WHAT HAPPENED?

The first thing you have to remember is that all psychics and mediums are human, and they occasionally have an off day. As a medium, I need to be at my best when I'm doing a reading or an event, because connecting with the other side is very draining. That's why I have an "escape clause" in my agreement for private readings. It gives me the option to reschedule if I have a migraine or the flu. If I'm not well, it's going to reflect in the reading, and I always want to ensure that my clients have the best experience possible.

Sometimes even with an escape clause things can go sideways. For example, I was on a national tour when I came down with a kidney stone. People had waited months for the event, and the venue wouldn't allow me to reschedule. They gave me tons of meds and basically pushed me out onstage. Let me tell you, I was seeing a lot more than dead people on that tour!

Spirit still came through at that event, but I noticed the messages were a little jumbled, and the details weren't as accurate as usual. I don't think the audience noticed, but I did. I knew it wasn't my best.

Anything that affects my brain, like medication, sinus infections, or migraines, can affect my readings.

I don't let general things like being in a bad mood get in the way. If I'm arguing with my family or worried about something, I can put that aside. It wasn't always that way, but I've learned to allow myself a good half hour to get centered before an event. I wouldn't say I meditate, exactly, but I have my own technique for quieting my mind and getting focused. It's meditation, Matt Fraser–style.

Like any professional, I have my rituals to ensure I give my audience and clients what they came for. When I'm preparing to do a reading, I don't eat anything right before and just drink water or coffee. I definitely have a no-alcohol policy for myself on the day of a show. I never liked alcohol because it dulls my senses and that includes my psychic ability.

It's Not Me, It's You!

Sometimes I'm having a great day, and I feel like the readings are right on target, but the client isn't happy. That's usually because they don't realize that Spirit is in the driver's seat! Some people come to a reading with very specific expectations, it's as if they've planned the reading before it begins. They decide in their own head who they want to hear from and what kinds of things they want the soul to say. I have to break the news that it doesn't work that way. I'm not in control of what comes through, either. A medium can make a request, and most likely the person will come through. But souls in heaven have a mind of their own, and even the best medium can't force them to come through if they're not ready.

One more tip is that it's important to pick a medium that suits you from a personality perspective, and to be aware of their specialty. Yes, there are specialties! You might need a medium to connect with a deceased loved one, a psychic for guidance about your own life, a medical medium for health issues, or even a pet medium.

90 Percent Accuracy Is an A

A good psychic reading should be about 90 percent accurate. Hitting everything 100 percent is rare because the visions aren't always crystal clear. Things get switched up in translation. I might have a vision of your husband on a motorcycle, when he actually drove a moped. Everything is filtered through the medium, so it depends on their frame of reference. Maybe your grandmother is playing canasta, but I see that as bridge because I don't know all my card games!

Also, some spirits are not good communicators. If your dad never talked when he was alive, he won't have the gift of gab on the other side, so he may not be able to provide a medium with all the details needed for a clear reading.

Sometimes you may wonder, *What is this medium talking about?* Even if you don't understand what comes through, make notes during or after your reading. Some insights that didn't hit home when you first heard them, might make perfect sense in a few months.

The bottom line is, you have to trust the medium before booking your reading. Word of mouth is best, but if you can't get a reference, do your homework. Check out a prospective medium's website and trust your intuition.

WHAT IF MY LOVED ONE DOESN'T COME THROUGH IN A READING?

If the soul you want to connect with doesn't come through, don't think the worst. There are many different reasons your loved one isn't talking at that moment. This does not mean that the person has not made it to heaven, only that there were factors blocking the connection at that particular time and place. Here are the most common ones.

1. **The timing is wrong.** Usually that means it's too soon. When a soul passes, they go through something called a "spirit life review." This is a process of transition where the soul lets go of all the negative anger, grudges, and regrets they were holding on to here on earth. The whole process is like moving into a new apartment—they have to get everything settled before they are ready to communicate with you.

2. **Your grief is too fresh.** Spirit may try to reach you, but grief can be a wall between the dead and the living. Grief makes us question ourselves, our loved ones, and even our faith. Extreme grief closes you off emotionally and energetically, and that can be a problem. You have to be open and receptive for Spirit to come through.

3. **Their message won't help you.** Souls don't just drop in to say hello. Their goal is to deliver a message that helps you live a better life, gain closure, learn a lesson, or heal. If they don't have anything useful to say, or if they don't think you're in a position to benefit from their message, they'll wait for a better time. Their wish is that you are focused on living, not searching for them and building your life

around them. For that reason, they carefully consider the timing and value of their words before they share them.

Always remember that Spirit comes through because there's something they have to tell you. They will try to speak to you when you're struggling or faced with a challenge—or to finish an important conversation they didn't get to complete in this world.

If your loved one doesn't come through in a reading, it doesn't mean they're not with you. It just means they're waiting for the right time, for both of you, to speak up. They'll come through when the time is right; and while you're waiting, be on the lookout for signs that they're with you.

HOW LONG SHOULD I WAIT BETWEEN READINGS?

A reading is a good way to receive insights, tools, and information to help you improve your life, but I recommend you limit readings to every year or so. A reading will usually give you about a year's worth of information; but remember, you are meant to live your own life, not be guided 24/7 by the spirits.

Even though souls are all-seeing, they aren't there to give you all the answers! It is impossible to cheat life and always make the right decisions. We were designed to learn through trial and error. It's perfectly normal to be unsure, and occasionally make the wrong choice. Souls in heaven understand you have free will, and they want you to rely on yourself, first and foremost. When it is appropriate, they will give you insights, but they cannot make decisions for you. And they don't want to, because they know that won't help you to grow.

When someone you love dies, it's best to wait about a year before booking a session with a medium. Not only will the message be stronger, but you will be in a better place to receive it. If you can't wait or if your intuition is telling you there's something you need to hear, try attending a group reading instead of a private one. You may hear from that special someone, or you may hear from someone else in spirit who was near and dear to you. Even if you don't make a direct connection, you will walk away feeling inspired after witnessing the messages received by others. Rest assured, when the time is right, your loved one will come through with a very special message for you.

HOW DO I KNOW IF A PSYCHIC OR MEDIUM IS "THE REAL THING"?

If you're asking this question, it's likely something has already triggered your intuition to be wary. If you believe in mediumship but have doubts about a particular person—beware. This isn't the medium for you.

Use your intuition, do your homework, and trust your feelings. It's just like a first date. If red flags are popping up and you're feeling uneasy, move on!

Talking to a medium should feel like talking to an old friend, someone who "gets you." But at the same time, the medium should be focused on you. They shouldn't talk too much about themselves, and it shouldn't feel like they're trying to sell you something. Beware if a medium uses fear tactics by telling you there's a spell or a curse on you. That's usually followed by an upsell. I can't tell you how many people call me in a panic. "A medium told me I have a hex on me, and they want me to pay them to remove it." That's not just a red flag, it's a giant banner that reads BEWARE!

We just talked about the fact that one private reading a year is probably enough. A medium shouldn't string you along to sign you up for lots of readings. I believe in giving my clients all the information I'm getting, right then and there. Your loved one doesn't want you spending too much time with a medium. First, because they don't always have useful new information, and second, because they want you to live your own life.

A Medium's Mission

A medium also shouldn't make promises. Of course, they should be able to get you a message, but connecting with a soul is not an exact science. The soul determines if they will come through, not the medium.

If a medium has something for you, they should tell you. I gave a woman an amazing reading at an event. Afterward, another medium came up to her and said, "Your dad has more to tell you!" She gave the woman her card and wanted to charge her for more readings.

There are no "office hours" when you're a medium. If I see a spirit around someone at the market or Dunkin' Donuts and I feel it's important to make a connection, I'll go right up to that person and let them know. Of course, I'm always respectful of the person and make sure they're receptive to receiving a message, but there's no stringing them along. If they're willing, I'll deliver the message to them.

Sure, I have events and schedule readings for people, but my primary mission is to get the messages from Spirit to their loved ones, not to book new business.

CAN MY LOVED ONE FROM THE AFTERLIFE TELL ME WHO TO MARRY?

Your loved ones will never make decisions for you. They may guide you, but you have your own life to live and that includes making your own choices.

However, Spirit will sometimes come through and give you a heads-up about someone who will come into your life. They might even let you know how they feel about that person. But that's it. Whether you date or marry them is up to you.

I had a friend who came to me for advice. She was lonely and wanted to meet someone. But she was studying to be a nurse and was very dedicated. To make things even harder, she was not a party person, and had trouble making small talk because she was so driven and serious. She had no time for social gatherings, and when she made the time, she got discouraged because she didn't meet the right kind of people.

She came to a reading and wanted to know if she'd ever be in a romantic relationship. She was feeling hopeless, but her grandfather came through and told her she'd meet a person named Ryan, whom she would have a deep connection with. He told her she wasn't like other girls. She wasn't the kind of person to casually date lots of people. He reassured her, "When the right one comes, it will hit hard."

She wasn't totally buying it. She couldn't think of anyone named Ryan in her social circle. I told her, "Don't worry! Just wait."

A year later, I got a call from her. She was on cloud nine! She'd met a wonderful man named Ryan, and they were engaged.

Sometimes we lose hope, and our loved ones come through to keep us on track. They want us to be hopeful about the future, not discouraged.

However, there are some readings that aren't as clear cut as this one. You might meet multiple men or women before meeting your soul mate. Your grandfather might see you with a Steve—but he may or may not be your soul mate. Steve might just be a romantic partner you meet on the path to finding your true soul mate.

What really cracks me up is when I tell someone Spirit's prediction that they will meet someone, and they ask, "Will I like this person?"

Yes, they're seeing your future, not creating it. They're not arranging a marriage from the afterlife, although they might try to put someone in your path. Ultimately, the decision of who you will fall in love with is yours!

I do want to point out that I don't always get a name in a reading. The soul won't always give me a name, and it's not because they don't know. But in some cases, they feel you might be overly influenced by knowing that name. They don't want you to feel that every Nancy you meet is "the one."

I HAD A PSYCHIC READING AND THE PREDICTION DIDN'T COME TRUE. WHY?

There could be a lot of reasons why things don't turn out exactly as predicted, but (stop me if I've said this before) the main ones are free will and divine timing.

Sometimes the prediction does come true . . . but you get in the way!

There was a woman applying for a job. It was a big step up in her career, and she really wanted it. Her grandmother came through and said, *"Yes, you'll get the job!"* She applied and went on interview after interview. Finally, the company offered her the job. She was so happy, and the fact that her grandmother had predicted the new job made her confident. In fact, maybe she was a little too confident.

When it came to negotiating the details, the company wanted her to relocate and start work in two months. She wanted at least six months to get settled before she started, and wouldn't budge on her demand. Because of her reading, she didn't think she had to compromise! She was wrong, and they gave the job to the next candidate.

I got a call, and that's when she told me the whole story. She was really upset! Her grandmother came through and explained that she had in fact gotten the job, but she ruined her deal by not agreeing to the terms.

What her grandma had predicted was true, but free will—and maybe too much confidence—got in the way.

Timing Is Everything

Sometimes a prediction doesn't come true because of divine timing. A medium might predict that you will have a relationship with a girl you have a crush on. Based on that, you ask the girl out, but she never accepts your advances, and you end up friend-zoned. Then, ten years later at your class reunion, you might wind up together. For ten years, you thought the medium had been wrong, but she wasn't. You just didn't understand the timeline.

Time Is Different on the Other Side

That brings up a good point. With psychic readings, time is fluid. The future is always changing, and there are all kinds of influences that can affect the outcomes. Use your reading as a guide, and don't expect to get an exact schedule of events.

For example, in my family, my mom gives the family a reading as a little gift or surprise. Being that my mom is a life reader, she primarily sees life events, milestones, and accomplishments. What we've learned to do is to create a psychic checklist from our reading! We write down everything she says. Everyone in my family has four to five pages of predictions from my mom.

The other night, Alexa decided to pull out her reading checklist. Every time she checked something off, she'd write down the date. Going over her list, she noticed that some predictions happened right away, and others took years to manifest. We both found it interesting to see how my mom's predictions had unfolded over time.

While Alexa was going over her list, I decided to take out some of my own notes from my first ever medium reading with the medium who had started me on my journey. Almost twelve years later, some things that medium told me are still taking place.

HOW CAN I IMPROVE MY CHANCES OF MY LOVED ONE COMING THROUGH AT A GROUP EVENT?

There's no guarantee you'll be selected for a reading when you go to a group event, but one thing's for sure, whatever happens, you'll leave feeling more connected to your loved one in heaven.

So, keeping in mind that Spirit is in the driver's seat, there are a few things to remember when you attend your next group reading (in-person or online):

Go Ahead and Sit Anywhere

Some people feel they need to be in the front row, but a live mediumship demonstration is not a rock concert. My tickets are usually the same price, and there's a reason for that.

When you come to a reading, don't worry about where you are in the room, because it absolutely doesn't matter where you sit. If your loved one has a message, they will find you. I have had messages for people sitting at the back of a room as often as I've had them for people in the front row. The important thing is to come to the event with an open heart and a positive attitude.

Each event is a group experience, and every seat is a good seat. I might get pulled to the way back corner to deliver a message to a mother who lost her son. Later, I might be pulled to the middle of a row to talk to a woman who lost her sister. Going in, I never know where the messages will be going, all I know is to listen and follow the direction of Spirit.

Be Mindful and Patient

When your loved one has a message for you, that message will come when the time is right. Messages from heaven don't always come when we want them to or when we think they should. The messages come when we need them to and when we are supposed to receive them. And when I say "be mindful," there's a good reason for that. If you're too focused on what you want, you might miss an important insight from another person's reading that could help you in your own life.

Remember that time doesn't matter. If your loved one passed recently, that doesn't make it any more likely you will hear from them. Many times, souls who passed years ago come through the strongest. If you don't get a message during a reading, that doesn't mean your loved one doesn't want to talk to you. The time might not be right, or there could be other souls who have a more urgent message for someone in the room.

Bring Memories, Not Memorabilia

Belongings don't really help when it comes to receiving a message at a group reading. Your loved ones are connected to you. To your loved ones in heaven, the memories and soul connection you share are much more important than any physical objects. The physical objects are great for helping *you* feel the connection, but they don't matter to the medium, or to your loved ones. Bring them if they make you feel good, but remember, the connection is in your heart, not in your hands.

Have an Open Mind and an Open Heart

Sometimes you might attend an event hoping to hear a message from your mom, but your dad comes through instead. It depends on who has something meaningful to say. You might even get a message from someone you don't like or didn't even want to hear from. Sometimes an ex-husband will come through with a message to apologize for bad behavior. It's so important to keep an open mind and be receptive to whatever comes your way.

One last thing. Keep your eyes and ears open after an event. Hearing the messages and feeling the energy in the room is so powerful that many people report noticing signs and feeling their loved ones extra strongly for weeks afterward. You may also find yourself thinking about a reading someone else received, and realize that in some way, that message also applies to you.

SHOULD I BRING ANY OF MY LOVED ONE'S BELONGINGS TO A MEDIUM?

If you're getting a reading from me, there's no need to bring watches, photos, keys, or anything else. But it actually depends on the medium. Remember, all mediums connect to Spirit differently, so it might help some to hold a personal item.

For me, the way I sense or feel Spirit is that I see the departed behind the person I'm meant to read for. When I see the soul standing there, I know I have to go over there and deliver a message.

I've had people bring ashes, photos, hair—one woman brought her husband's glass eye. None of it really helped me connect with their loved one's spirit.

Sometimes people believe bringing a photo or personal item will give them an edge, or maybe help them catch the medium's eye. I'll never forget the time I was hosting a reading, and I asked one row of people to stand up. I could clearly see a spirit standing behind a couple and their teen-age children. I zeroed in on the spirit coming through, and as I was giving the family their message, I kept feeling something behind me, and it was kicking me. I didn't know what the heck was going on! I looked around, and a woman from the audience was whacking me in the back with her father's cowboy boot. She had brought the boot, and during the whole event kept waving it and holding it up in the air—and finally she kicked me with it! I guess she was doing these bizarre things to get my attention, or maybe get the attention of her father on the other side! I really don't know what she was thinking. But he didn't have a message for her, and all the boots in the world were not going to bring him through.

But no matter how many times I say it, people will always try this stuff. People tap me with items as I walk down the aisles, they hold up pictures, and one woman brought a balloon with her husband's face on it to an event. That balloon did catch my eye, but it didn't bring her husband through.

ARE YOU EVER WRONG IN A READING?

Of course I've been wrong. I'm human and I make mistakes. As I've said, Spirit is never wrong, but there are times when I don't relay a message correctly. Messages aren't always exact, and as I've said, there are a few things that can muddy the waters with a reading. Timing can be an issue, and so can the medium's own interpretation of signs and images.

When the Time Is Right, the Message Will Make Sense

When I think about messages that felt wrong but turned out not to be, this one always comes to mind. Once, Alexa was competing in the Miss Rhode Island pageant. This pageant had an adult competition and a teenage one. Alexa was in the adult class. I wasn't trying to predict Alexa's pageant, because it was just too close to home, so I focused on the teenage pageant. During the teen division, the girls came out onstage, and there was one in particular who stood out to me. The minute I saw her, I had a crystal-clear vision of her crying onstage, being crowned Miss Teen Rhode Island. I told my family she was going to win, and I sat back in my chair to watch my prediction come true—only to be completely wrong! The girl I predicted made it to the top five, but she was nowhere near being the winner.

I came home and told Alexa what happened. I was so puzzled because Spirit is never wrong, and I couldn't figure out how I could have misinterpreted such a vivid vision. After a little while I brushed it off and didn't worry too much about it.

The next year, Alexa entered the pageant again. The teenage girl was there, too, and this time when they called the winner, it was her! My whole vision from the previous year came flooding back to me. She was onstage, people were applauding, she was holding her flowers and crying. It was just as I'd pictured it. I realized my prediction was correct, but the timeline was not what I'd expected.

What does all this mean when you're the person getting a reading? When you go to a medium, keep an open mind. Remember that the medium is piecing together images, words, impressions, and even physical feelings in their own body. Don't push too hard to try to make the message fit, but *do* remember that the timing or details might not be exactly what you expect. Remember their words, and even write down some notes. What doesn't seem right to you during a reading, might make perfect sense in a few weeks, months, or even years!

GOING DEEPER

Finding the Answers Within Yourself

Mediums talk to souls on the other side, but when there's no medium around, call upon your angels! Call upon loved ones in heaven! If your mom was the person whom you talked to about relationships, she can still help. In fact, she'd love nothing more.

Here are some of the angels most commonly called upon, and what they "specialize" in.

- When you think of protection, Archangel Michael probably comes to mind. He guards you from negative energy, accidents, and illness. Archangel Michael is always there to shelter you and provide the love energy when you need it.

- Archangel Raphael is a healing angel. He can help you recover from sickness or injury, and is also the angel to call upon when you're depressed or experiencing emotional trauma. If you or someone you love is sick, lost, or struggling, you can ask for his assistance with a silent request or prayer.

- If you are a student or have an important decision to make, you can call on Archangel Uriel. Uriel is the angel you go to when you're looking for understanding, information, or a wise head to help with a difficult choice. Just invite him in, ask your question, and he will share his divine wisdom with you!

- Archangel Ariel is the angel associated with animals. You can call upon her for guidance and healing for your furry or feathered friends.

- If you're a writer, teacher, or speaker, you'll find Archangel Gabriel an invaluable source of support and inspiration in the areas of communication and creativity.

It's rare to actually see an angel, wings and all, so how do you know when you're getting guidance, encouragement, and protection from a divine source? The answer is pretty simple: listen to your heart. If you feel a warm, safe sensation, or feel yourself being guided by a being who wants only what's best for you—guess what? Angels are with you!

Oh, and one final thing. When you ask for an angel's help—either for helping you get your dream job, healing from an illness, or just finding your car keys—and they deliver, don't forget to send up a little prayer of thanks. Even angels like being appreciated!

CHAPTER 7

Love and Relationships

*"You may have many partners in life,
but only one is your true soul mate."*

IF MY FIANCÉ PASSED BEFORE
WE WERE MARRIED, WILL WE BE
REUNITED IN HEAVEN?

This question came from a reading I did not too long ago.

Don't Worry About the Paperwork . . .

A woman named Jessica came to my event after a heartbreaking experience. Her fiancé had tragically passed right before their wedding day. She was devastated, but she felt even worse when a relative told her that since the marriage hadn't been blessed in a church, the two would not be together in heaven.

Luckily, her fiancé came through to set everyone straight. He assured Jessica he was watching over her every day, and that as a spirit, he could see their future. He wanted her to live her life and continue her journey, but know that they would be reunited in the afterlife. Confident that he was her true soul mate, he urged her to date and love other people.

Even though Jessica didn't want to be with anyone else, she eventually ended up marrying her fiancé's best friend. She was convinced there would never be another man like him, but her new husband was so much like him that marrying him was the next best thing. They both found comfort and a different kind of love with each other, and together they kept his memory alive.

The last thing her fiancé asked me to communicate to Jessica was that his greatest wish was for her to live her life to the fullest, knowing that they would be together in eternity.

This proves what I have said over and over. They don't check for marriage certificates or divorce papers in heaven. All decisions come down to the soul. Souls that share a deep connection in this world and are truly in love will always end up together in heaven.

Jessica's fiancé wasn't worried, because he knew they'd be reunited in the end. Until then, he didn't want her to miss out on the things they'd planned to do together. It's clear from this that there's no jealousy in heaven, which brings us to our next question.

IS MY DECEASED HUSBAND UPSET THAT I'M DATING SOMEONE ELSE?

It's a little difficult to understand this because we imagine our loved one approaching their experience in heaven as they did life in the physical world. The fact is, now that they're in heaven, they view things with a different perspective.

People don't carry jealousy or resentment with them when they die. There's just no room for heavy emotions like that in heaven.

Regardless of how they behaved in life, in heaven, souls come from a place of love.

That can be difficult for their loved ones on earth to understand.

Your Soul Mate Wants One Thing— For You to Be Happy!

I remember doing a reading for a woman whose husband had been very jealous when he was alive. He wanted his wife all to himself and wouldn't even let her have male friends. Unfortunately, he also had addiction issues, and he passed at a very young age. Despite his flaws, his wife had loved him deeply and fell into a depression after his death, thinking of all the plans that would never be realized and the things they would never be able to do together.

She lived her life as if he were still alive, and didn't speak to or look at other men.

She came to me for a reading, and her husband immediately came through. Looking back with his heavenly perspective, he realized that because of his addiction, he'd robbed her of the life she had dreamed of. He told her he'd be sending her an old friend who she would have a relationship with.

The reading went sideways from there!

The woman freaked out. "That's not my husband! He'd never want me to even look at another man!"

She simply couldn't understand that from his new vantage point, he could see more clearly. He explained that it wasn't her fault he'd died. He had made a choice, and now he wanted to make things right.

She had a hard time believing this.

It took me (with help from her husband) some time to turn her around. Finally, these words got through to her. "I am in peace in heaven. I have no pain—so why would I want you to live in pain every day?"

I often wonder what happens to my clients after we part ways, and in the following case, I found out.

I ran into the woman years later. She was married and had a child, and looking back, she realized what a dark, unhappy place she'd been living in before our reading.

Even though she had a new husband and family, her first husband lived on in her heart. She was free to maintain a soul connection with him because she no longer felt he was judging her. Despite everything, he had been her true soul mate, and she was at peace knowing that in the next chapter, they would be together again.

We'll talk more about soul mates later, but just know that death is a transition, and it changes the way people look at things. Sometimes it's important to look at things through the eyes of your loved one in heaven. Know that they want the very best for you and are no longer driven by earthly emotions like anger and jealousy.

DO GAY COUPLES END UP TOGETHER?

Spirit has taught me that love is love no matter what. Love knows no gender, race, or religion. I've talked to many souls who were gay, and if they were soul mates on earth, they knew they would be reunited in heaven.

However, the idea that love has no limits is still a lesson that needs to be embraced in this world.

Just as humans let go of jealousy and anger when they pass, sometimes their other views change when they get to the other side.

A Heavenly Shift

For example, I recently had a client who was afraid to marry his partner because it went against his mother's belief system. His mom was so against same-sex marriage that he never told her he was gay, and he definitely never mentioned that he was in a committed relationship with another man. The two had many conversations where he tried to open her mind, but she refused to change.

So reluctantly, he continued to keep his personal life a secret.

When his mother passed, my client's partner thought that they would finally be able to get married. But as much as he wanted to, he still couldn't do it. Even though his mom was no longer alive, he thought he knew how she would feel about that.

When he came to me, he brought up another concern. His mother's passing had gotten him thinking about love and heaven and the afterlife. He wanted reassurance that he and his boyfriend would be together in heaven.

When his mom came through in the reading, he was shocked by what she had to say.

She had gained a whole new perspective on the other side. Looking back, she could see how he'd concealed his sexual orientation because of her. She realized how much her judgment had hurt him, and she regretted that her opinions had kept him from being true to himself. Now that she was in heaven, she could see how she'd selfishly pushed him to live the life she wanted, not the life that would make him happy.

His mother then shared her deepest regret—that she had never met his partner. She didn't want him to lose out on his chance to experience love.

During the reading, she gave the couple her blessing and encouraged them to get married.

This reading proved that it's never too late to change your mind or heal a misunderstanding. It gave him the clarity he needed to move on. He told me he loved her more and could fully honor her memory, knowing she had finally accepted him.

The moral of the story: don't assume your loved ones have the same prejudices and beliefs after they pass that they did when they were alive. Heaven teaches them the importance of love over everything. So go ahead and follow your heart, and know your loved one in heaven is cheering you on!

DO ALL COUPLES END UP TOGETHER IN HEAVEN?

I'll tell you if you promise not to freak out. The answer is no! Every time I say this, people start to panic. More often than not, married couples who were in love on earth, end up together in heaven. But it's important to remember it's the soul connection that counts, not the marriage license.

As we all know, not everyone marries for love.

I've done many readings when couples were very unhappy together before one of them passed, but they stayed married for the kids. Some marriages are arranged by families, based on their cultural beliefs, and some people marry for other reasons, like money or security.

They might find comfort in the relationship, but they are not soul mates.

Sometimes Family Doesn't Know Best

A woman came to me whose husband had passed. They'd had an arranged marriage, but unlike many such marriages where the couple grows to love each other, these two never found happiness together. Their life was lived in an effort to please their families, but the longer they were together, the more they realized they just didn't have a connection.

Rather than let their families down, they lived separate lives in the same house. They slept in different rooms, had no intimacy, their jobs were on different schedules. Basically, they barely saw each other—but they were married, at least on paper.

But that wasn't enough. As the marriage went on, the pressure from their families grew. They were pressured to have children, but bringing children into this loveless household didn't feel right to either of them.

Anytime someone brought up children, the two would feel nothing but anxiety.

Meanwhile, the husband started having issues at work, and the resulting financial burdens just put more pressure on the couple.

They were getting pressure from every side. Because of the stress he was under, the husband developed a panic disorder. My client didn't know how to help him, because they didn't have an emotional connection. They had never learned to support each other in this world.

Eventually, life got to be too much for him, and he passed by suicide. After he died, my client was left with such heavy burdens. She looked back over her life and questioned everything. She felt she could have saved him, and because of her guilt, she committed herself to a life alone until she could make it up to him in heaven.

He came through and told her they were never soul mates. He wished he had the courage when he was alive to follow his heart and do what was right for both of them.

He released her from the guilt she'd been carrying, and from the relationship itself, and encouraged her to go out and find her true soul mate.

It wasn't until he passed and came through in the reading that they had an honest conversation and admitted to each other that their souls were not compatible.

She felt so relieved. Her whole life had felt wrong, but she couldn't really validate her feelings until that reading. After that, she was free to find her soul mate and experience what love truly was.

This is an example of a couple that was not destined to be together in heaven—and shouldn't have been.

IF I HAD MULTIPLE PARTNERS, WHICH ONE WILL I END UP WITH?

Who do you think I am? Jerry Springer? Every time I get this question, things become very confusing for me and for the person I'm reading for. Here's a dramatic example.

I recently had a ninety-year-old woman attend an event with her family. Her backstory was pretty unusual. Because of her longevity, she'd outlived two husbands and a boyfriend. She had loved them all and enjoyed a special and unique relationship with each one.

They felt the same about her. Each of them came through and shared different stories and experiences and told me how much they loved her.

At the very end of the reading, she asked me which of them she'd be with in heaven. Her first husband came through and said he'd greet her when it was her time to pass. He would bring her to heaven, and they would be together.

She was with her family, and I expected them all to be equally pleased to hear this. That wasn't exactly the case. The minute I told her she'd be with husband number one, her daughters were so happy. But when I looked at her, she wasn't smiling! "Oh no, I didn't want him.

Don't get me wrong, he cared for me, and we had a wonderful family and a great life together. But nobody was like my last boyfriend. He was really hot stuff, and that's who I was hoping I'd be with in heaven." Her comment took us all by surprise, and I hated to disappoint her, but I had to be straight with her. I explained that her boyfriend had previously had a wife of his own, and that woman was his true soul mate.

I reassured her that everything gets worked out when you pass, and to enjoy the rest of her life and not to dwell on what was in store for her in heaven. She agreed to be grateful for the love connection they'd all shared and to just let things play out.

That reading made me just a little uncomfortable, because I'd always rather tell people what they want to hear. But as much as I hate disappointing anyone, I always tell the truth, and have learned to trust what Spirit tells me.

So, final note—the very next year that woman was in my audience again—this time in the front row. I walked up to her thinking she wanted to hear from her husband again. Turns out that in the past year, she'd met a *new* man she liked even better than the previous three. She was in her nineties and still going strong!

Just as I've learned to trust what Spirit tells me, people have to trust that their experience in heaven will be exactly as it's meant to be. When you go to heaven, your soul mate will be there, and you'll feel that beautiful connection for eternity.

HOW CAN I RAISE MY KIDS WITHOUT MY HUSBAND/WIFE?

This is a tough question that has a very simple answer. Spirit always tells me to remind people of the love their partner had for their children before they left this world. So many times, when a loved one passes away, the parent left to raise the kids wonders how their spouse would have reacted to various situations. They try to take the deceased parent into account as they guide and teach the children. There's nothing wrong with that as long as it doesn't make the living parent second-guess themselves, but it's really not necessary.

Loved Ones Are Forever in Our Hearts

What Spirit really wants is for you to simply keep the memory of the missing parent alive. If the children were too young to have strong memories of the parent they've lost, it's important to find ways to introduce the children to them.

Spirit has taught me that when a family member passes while children are young, it's important to teach them about their relationship with souls in the afterlife, and how their loved ones are always with them. Creating special traditions can help your kids to feel a connection with a parent or a grandparent who has passed on.

The Power of the "Grammy Pouch"

My first date with my wife, Alexa, was at a small coffee shop in Rhode Island. At the time, her grandmother was the only person in her life she had ever lost. While I was sitting with her, her grandmother appeared and told me Alexa was carrying a small pouch that had belonged to her beloved "Grammy."

When I told Alexa, she looked shocked! She reached into her pocketbook and pulled out a small pouch. "It's the Grammy pouch my family put together when she died." Inside the pouch was a photo, her grandmother's prayer medals, and some small pieces of jewelry. The family passed the pouch around to anyone who needed a little extra support. It went to a grandson who was taking the bar exam, and a granddaughter who was graduating high school. What's truly amazing was that it was there when Alexa met me. I felt as if I was not just meeting Alexa but meeting her grandmother at the same time.

Spirit tells me that if we keep our loved one's memory alive for our children and future generations, we never really lose them.

Bottom line, the answer to the question is this: You don't have to raise the kids without your spouse, their grandparents, or any member of your family. If you keep their memory alive, they'll always be with you and their children.

IF I MOVE OUT OF MY HOME, WILL MY HUSBAND OR WIFE'S SPIRIT FOLLOW ME?

You can't get away from them so easily! Remember, your loved one is connected to you, not where you're living. Wherever you currently are is where they will be.

Don't get me wrong, there are times when Spirit will visit places that held special memories like a vacation spot, or the place you met. But normally, what matters is that they stay close to you even if you're in another state, country, or outer space!

"I Love What You've Done with the Place!"

I once had neighbors who were absolutely soul mates in this world. They had met when they were young and were absolutely inseparable from then on. They believed in heaven and the afterlife and were very attuned to the spiritual world. After they had been married for many years, the wife became very ill. Knowing she would soon be passing, she told her husband that when she transitioned over to the spirit world, she didn't want him staying in the same apartment they currently lived in. She worried that if he stayed there, he'd become depressed and feel that the house was empty without her in it. She assured him that when she passed, wherever he decided to go, she would find him.

After she passed away, as hard as it was, he packed up his things and moved out of state to be closer to friends. He thought of her constantly and talked to her every day. As he was decorating the house, he found himself choosing similar colors and furnishings. It wound up looking a lot like the house where they had lived together. One night he was really missing her, and when he finally fell asleep, he had a dream about her. She was sitting in the living room of his new house. He could sense that she approved of where he was living now, and ever since that dream, he was able to sense and feel her in the new place.

He was happy he had moved and felt good to be on a new journey with her, not stuck in past memories.

This all comes back to the basic message I hear over and over from souls in heaven. They don't expect you to mourn endlessly and act like life is over because they are no longer alive. Their most sincere wish is that you live your best life, love again, and be happy. And even though you'll be reunited with your soul mate in heaven, they don't want you to spend your precious time on earth waiting for that. Just be at peace that what's meant to be will be, and when the time is right, you'll be together again.

WHAT IS A SOUL MATE?

A soul mate is your twin flame; someone your heart is connected with at the very deepest level. Some people believe soul mates have shared past lives. I don't know about that, but I do know you will carry that connection with you forever, whatever form your soul takes.

Don't Spend Time Worrying About Meeting Your Soul Mate

Meeting your soul mate isn't something that you need to "work on." It's totally possible and normal to enjoy a long, happy, and productive relationship with someone who is not your soul mate. You can be married and have children together and love each other. But that kind of relationship ends when you die, and you'll be with your true soul mate in heaven.

Don't spend too much time stressing over missing out on your great love. That's one of those things that can drive you crazy if you try to control it. You have to trust the universe. You might not reconnect with your husband or wife in heaven, but you will surely connect with your soul mate.

My grandpa's story illustrates this perfectly. He was in love with a girl he met when he was sixteen. He felt in his heart that she was his soul mate, but she was young and wound up choosing another man she believed could give her what she was looking for. Grandpa was brokenhearted, but eventually he met and married my grandmother.

Grandpa and his old flame went their separate ways, and both had beautiful families and children with their spouses. They didn't have contact again until almost fifty years from when they'd last been together. Both their spouses had passed, and they found themselves alone. As fate would have it, they ran into each other and picked up where they'd left off as teens.

They never regretted their marriages, but they were thankful to connect decades later. In their case, they didn't have to wait until they passed to be together—and I'm pretty confident their souls will be connected for all eternity.

IF YOU PASS ALONE, WILL YOU FIND YOUR SOUL MATE IN HEAVEN?

Not all soul mates meet in this world. It may be your destiny to be together, but you also have free will, and the choices you make might keep you and your soul mate from meeting. Your soul mate may pass early, or you may have children with someone else and never get together.

Sometimes you have a chance encounter and meet your soul mate, but for one reason or another you don't recognize them. A lot of people worry about this, but I assure them that this is an area where you have to trust the universe!

Love at Long Last!

I once did a reading for the daughter of a woman who had gotten pregnant as a teenager. Because the woman and her boyfriend were both so young when they became parents, he wound up leaving, and she was left to raise their daughter alone. The woman focused on her responsibilities as a mom, and never got married. But as her life went on and her daughter grew older, the woman yearned for love. All she wanted in life was to be in a relationship and have a partner who truly cared about her. No matter how hard she tried, her soul mate eluded her. She wound up in many relationships that weren't right for her. Some were emotionally abusive, and some just ended quickly without going anywhere.

Her daughter had watched her mother suffer for years as she searched for love. The daughter found a wonderful husband, but she felt guilty that her mother never experienced that same kind of love. When her mother passed, the thought of the sacrifices she had made during her life brought the daughter great pain.

She was heartbroken at the thought that her mother would never have the kind of romantic relationship she had longed for.

Her mom came through in the reading, and to her daughter's surprise, she had found her soul mate in heaven! He was someone she had known in high school, but first her pregnancy had kept them apart, and then he had passed unexpectedly a few years later.

All that was behind them, and when they met in heaven decades later, they were able to experience the beautiful soul connection they had been missing when they were alive.

I can't stress enough that meeting (or not meeting) your soul mate while you're alive is not something you can always control. Think of it like this. You and your soul mate are on a path toward each other, and destiny says you should meet. However, free will and other factors can knock one or both of you off the path and keep you from connecting. If you're meant to be together, your paths will cross in heaven and you'll be reunited in love for eternity!

WILL MY WIFE BE OLDER THAN ME IN HEAVEN?

This is one of those things that makes perfect sense when you think about it for a minute. Imagine if your soul mate died in their twenties, but you didn't pass until you were ninety-five. That could be very awkward when you are finally reunited in heaven. But fortunately, as I mentioned in chapter five, you don't have to worry about that because age is an earthly measurement, and all souls are ageless.

Our bodies are what age, not our souls. The soul is infinite, and that's what's waiting for you in heaven.

I've said before that there are no birthdays in heaven. Years are something that you keep track of on earth. As a human being, you're always looking toward the next milestone. Maybe you're excited to turn twenty-one, or dreading turning fifty. Either way, you're tracking time. Once you die, that stops because you've arrived at your destination, and that's that.

Don't worry. There's no need to get Botox before you pass! There will be no age difference, and age won't be an issue when you're reunited with your soul mate in heaven.

GOING DEEPER
Creating and Finding Love

You've probably heard me, and a lot of other people, talk about the power of positive thinking and setting intentions. One way to make that power work for you is to create a vision board of what you want. When it comes to finding a soul mate, I'm a BIG believer in this, because I credit my vision board for my own relationship with Alexa.

When it comes to love, creating a vision board serves a couple of purposes. First, it helps you to focus on what you really want in a relationship, so you stop wasting time pursuing the wrong people. Also, it sends a strong signal out to the universe. So while you're going through your day, your guides and angels are slowly working behind the scenes, making things happen!

As you create your board, make sure you're in a good place! Be calm and avoid distractions. I'd turn off your phone and computer so you don't get interrupted. It's all about listening to your heart and your intuition when creating the board. Oh, and this isn't a team effort, so don't let anyone help you—this is personal.

If you've never put together a vision board, it's easy. You can create one on your computer, but personally, I like going "old school" with my vision boards, and using poster board, scissors, and a glue stick. Pull together photos, images from magazines, and words that you're attracted to. Don't overthink it, but don't glue everything down until you've collected more images than you need to fill your board. Once you have your images, think about your soul mate, your ideal person. Now start arranging your material on the board. See which images feel right, and discard the ones that don't fit or resonate. For example, when I created my own "soul mate board" I had pictures of pageant girls, and women with dark hair and eyes. I had animals and travel photos—because I knew I wanted a warm woman who loved animals and had a sense of adventure. When the board was done, I found myself so sure of what I was looking for that when Alexa came along, there was no doubt she was the one.

One last thought—hang on to that glue stick! Know that you are constantly changing. Your goals change, your interests and hobbies change, and your board will change too. Update your board, but unless something drastic happens, don't replace it. Your old dreams will still be there in the background, mingling with the new!

Put your board in a place where you can see it, as a reminder to set a daily intention to find love and happiness. When you know what you want and are sending that love energy out into the universe, the next step is to wait and let the manifesting begin!

CHAPTER 8

I'm Not Afraid of Ghosts: Hauntings, Bad Deeds, and Negative Souls

"Light will always win over darkness."

SHOULD I BE WORRIED ABOUT EVIL SPIRITS?

Unfortunately, just as there are negative people here on earth, there are evil spirits on the other side. But the good news is that if you're reading this, it's unlikely you'll ever come in contact with one. True evil feeds off darkness and isolation, so stay in the light! If you don't go looking for evil, it's very rare that it will come looking for you.

There's not one evil spirit for every person who has done bad deeds on earth. Fortunately, there are way fewer! Even when they have things to atone for (and who doesn't?), almost all souls are able to cross over successfully. Before they enter heaven, they have the opportunity to make things right. However, if their acts are really bad and they don't have the desire to make amends, they can get "stuck" and may be unable to move on. You might wonder, when a soul is stuck, where are they?

Evil Hides in the Darkness

Have you noticed how old, abandoned places are usually the ones that are haunted in scary movies? It's not just that way in film. That's actually the environment these spirits are attracted to. The last place they want to be is around sunshine and happy families. They'd much rather hide out in the shadows.

I personally never go looking for haunted houses and evil spirits. The only people I know who have run-ins with negative spirits are ghost hunters and paranormal explorers. The average person won't stumble across one at the supermarket or on their way to work.

That being said, I wouldn't be a psychic medium if I didn't have a good ghost story!

The Haunted Hotel Room

I had one experience with an evil spirit that was really quite creepy. A spirit won't haunt places where people are having a good time, like a crowded casino lobby, but that doesn't keep them out of other places in a casino.

I do a lot of events at casinos, and I have gotten to know many of the people who work there. One day a casino manager called me, totally freaked out! Crazy stuff had been happening in one of his rarely used hotel rooms. This room was kept empty because it was in a noisy spot next to the laundry and it overlooked the parking lot. Because it was so unpopular with guests, the room was used for storage and hadn't been occupied for years.

Now, think about a casino. Some of the larger ones, like this one, service thousands of guests a day. It would stand to reason, then, that a few people are bound to pass over while there.

One day the casino was completely booked up, and someone was desperate for a room. Management decided to clear out and make use of the noisy room.

When they sent a maid up to the room, she called maintenance right away. She couldn't get the chill out of the room. She'd cranked up the heat, and the thermostat read seventy degrees, but still the room was freezing. Maintenance sent someone up, but before they got there, the room suddenly warmed up.

They brushed aside the issue with the room's temperature and sent the guest up. A few minutes later, she called the front desk. "My room is freezing, and it smells like rotten eggs!"

Maintenance came again. When they got there, the temperature was normal, and the smell was gone.

Puzzled, the guest shrugged it off and went to dinner, but when she came back to unpack, she saw a cloud of smoke, which materialized as a dark figure moving around the room. This time she wasn't going to take any chances! She demanded to switch rooms because she said her room was haunted.

Still in need of the space, they booked another guest into the room. He was a big burly guy, and it didn't seem like anything would bother him. Wrong! The front desk called the manager in a panic when guest number two came running down in his underwear, swearing that something had pulled the sheets off him.

The manager couldn't figure out what the heck was happening, so he sent housekeeping to clean the room and get the guest's things, because the man was too terrified to enter the room again.

This time, housekeeping not only smelled the eggs but saw strange black smoke form into the shape of a man.

That's when I got the call. "Matt, *please* come get rid of this ghost!"

It was actually easier than you might think, to put this spirit in its place. The manager escorted me up to the room, along with a couple of security guards. Together, we turned on the lights, opened up the doors and windows, and I demanded that the spirit leave. I also brought sage, an herb that can be burned to help purify a space and cleanse the energy.

We walked the room together, while I burned the sage and spoke to the spirit: "This isn't your place; it's time to go." It took a few minutes for the energy to shift. The room had been feeling stifling and claustrophobic, then, in an instant, it felt light and airy.

My instructions to the manager to keep the place clear were not what you would think. "Book this room as much as possible! Now that the bad tenant is gone, keep the room filled, to keep it from returning."

The manager started booking the room at a reduced rate. Now the room is in regular rotation, and there hasn't been an incident since.

A good rule to remember is that positive energy pushes out negative energy. That's why you won't see evil spirits at Disneyland or shopping malls. There are too many happy people there. My advice is to listen to your gut, stay in the light, and avoid any space that gives you the creeps!

CAN SOMEONE PUT A SPELL ON YOU?

The answer is no—and to be honest, this question gets me kind of upset. You wouldn't believe how often people call me saying another psychic or medium has told them they have to pay to remove a spell or curse. If there's one thing spirit has taught me it's that no one—living or dead—can take over your life unless you let them. You have free will and complete control of your destiny. However, I think the reason some people believe in spells is because they can feel negative energy. But negative energy and spells are two totally different things.

For example, have you ever walked into a room after people were fighting and felt the bad energy lingering in the air?

Or maybe you were arguing with someone over text or email, and you can physically feel the emotion in the typed words, even though you're both miles apart.

Negative energy is really rough because it sticks around. If someone is angry or thinking bad thoughts about you, it can affect you—no matter where you are. You might not even know the person. It doesn't matter, just being in someone's thoughts can have an impact. This is due to the fact that we are spiritual, energetic beings, and we can sense and feel energy that's connected to us in any way.

Now, you're probably wondering why I'm saying this after I just said no one can cast a spell on you or control you. Don't get me wrong, some people do practice spells—but what is a spell? It's literally someone sending out energy. And here's the thing: even though you can feel bad energy, you don't have to let it in. It can't hurt you or affect you unless you allow it to, and the best shield against negativity is positivity.

It's like dealing with a schoolyard bully who backs right off when you confront him. When you decide negative thoughts and energy have no control over you, you take away the power!

The Spell Is Coming from Inside Your Mind

I had a client who was convinced an old friend was putting a spell on her. She was completely scared because she felt as if she'd lost control over her life. Her friend was very negative and would taunt her on social media and even text her and tell her she was sending her negative energy. My client was totally psyched out. She started blaming the woman for everything bad that happened in her life.

She came to me for a reading, and as soon as I tapped into her energy, I could feel the negativity. But it wasn't a spell. It was her own belief that her friend had control over her. I felt the fear and paranoia flooding her body, and I knew this problem could be easily solved if she would just change her own mindset.

I talked to the spirits, and they advised me that the best way to combat the energy was to block it and send it back.

"Block her on social and on your phone. Get rid of the things that remind you of that person. Just focus on your own energy. And take all that negative energy coming at you and imagine "throwing it back.""

This proves my point, that you have to keep your own sense of who you are and maintain your own energetic boundaries. If you have strong boundaries, other people's "spells" or negative thoughts bounce right off you.

It's like a relationship. You have to protect who you are—keep your friends, beliefs, and the things that you enjoy—not give control of your identity to your partner.

Energy is like a simple math equation. When you subtract the negativity out of your life, you make room for more positivity to be added. And that positivity fills the space, energetically, and makes it hard for the negativity to return.

ARE EVENTS IN LIFE PREDESTINED?

The answer to this question is yes and no. Spirit has shown me that we are destined to meet certain people and receive certain opportunities. But we also have free will, and we make our own choices.

Your life is filled with gifts and opportunities. Your gifts are who you are and what you're good at. The opportunities are associated with the choices you make and the people you encounter.

The universe gives everyone different gifts. There are naturally talented healers, teachers, artists, psychics, etcetera, and all have certain things predestined for them. It's like Christmas—there will be gifts that have your name on them. Those are the experiences and opportunities that you will have here in this world. Sometimes it's not time for those gifts to be opened, but even if you veer off your path, your gift is always there waiting for the time to be right for you to open it.

I'm a perfect example of this. When I was growing up, I pushed my mediumship away, but no matter how many times I made another choice, my gift was still there, waiting for me. I just had to be in the right place to make good use of it.

You Get More Than One Chance!

Another thing Spirit has taught me is if something is meant to be, it will come back around—like the brass ring on a merry-go-round. If anyone tells me they "missed their big chance," I always reassure them that if it was right, it will come back.

Some things are excluded—illnesses or tragedies aren't predestined, they're just part of living an earthly life. The spiritual side of us can learn from those events, but they're not "meant to be." We are spiritual beings, and while we're here to learn and grow, we aren't sent here to suffer.

Spirit has a way of sending us signs, or even pushing us away from decisions that will end badly. That's when it's important to listen to your gut.

The Wrong Choice, at the Wrong Time

I had a chance to be part of an international event. Even though I'd been pursuing this opportunity, when the time came, I couldn't bring myself to sign onto it.

As I was trying to figure out what was holding me back, I was on the phone sharing my vague misgivings about the event with a friend, when I heard a voice that said, "Don't go!" The voice was distorted, and I wasn't 100 percent sure I heard it right.

That night I was determined to get to the bottom of it. I meditated and asked my guides what was happening.

The answer came quickly. I was told this wasn't the time. Spirit told me that another opportunity would follow, and it was okay to follow my intuition and say no.

They told me that heaven doesn't give us things only to take them away, so not to worry that I was missing out on a career opportunity.

I figured out what was holding me back. At the time, this trip wasn't right for me. I would have had to leave the country for six months. As soon as I said no, other opportunities came through locally—and they were even better! I knew then that leaving the country would have kept me from them.

The Right Place—the Wrong Time

Sometimes you just know something is meant to be, but then it doesn't happen! I was trying to purchase a home, and I was searching the internet for listings of homes for sale, when one place completely caught my eye. I called my Realtor, and the moment I walked in I knew this would be my house. I told the Realtor, "I want it!" I was *sure* it was all going to work out, but the Realtor came back and said there was a pending offer.

"No worries, I'm a psychic medium," I said. "The offer will fall through!"

"No way," she said. "It's a cash offer."

"We'll see about that! Call me when it falls through."

When the offer didn't fall through, I was shocked and a little depressed—and not just because I didn't get the house. I couldn't believe my intuition was wrong.

I put the whole thing out of my mind and kept living my life until six months later when the house was back on the market!

I couldn't believe it! I went back into the house, and it was crazy. The owners had moved in and started renovating the house, but within six months, he and his wife separated, and he didn't want to live there anymore.

I picked up where he left off with the remodel and moved in. I'm still living there.

Even though the initial disappointment made me doubt my intuition, the new development proved that what is meant to be, will be. You just might have to be patient.

It's experiences like this that make me trust the universe. If something feels meant to be but it's not happening, give it time. Heaven will make sure everything lines up when the time is right.

IS THERE SUCH A THING AS HELL?

The good news is that I've never done a reading where the soul was in hell. But I have done readings—and it is rare—when the person is unreachable. That makes me wonder if they are in a different place. I have talked to Spirit about this, and they have shown me that there are not two actual worlds like we see in movies or read about in books.

But there are souls who have made the amends necessary and moved on, and some that are still working things out. Until they have successfully transitioned, I can't connect with them.

Maybe another reason I don't connect with negative spirits is because I don't "invite them in." Before I do a reading, I set a positive intention and say I only want to talk to souls who are coming from the light and a place of love. There's truth to the fact that if you go looking for negativity you can find it. But I do the opposite.

Sometimes when I'm reaching out to souls I get a "try again later," but sometimes it's like I have hit a brick wall where I'll never reach them. That's when I know something is up that's beyond my ability to handle.

If there's a soul that's pure evil, I don't try to connect, or find out where they are. That's taken care of by God.

I like to think of the souls who are stuck here as being in a "time out," and they have the chance to redeem themselves when they realize the error of their ways.

WHAT'S FLUFFY LOOKING AT?

Can your dog or cat sense the presence of spirits? Absolutely! Pets have a sixth sense that allows them to see and communicate with souls who have passed on.

It's very common for dogs to bark at the chair their owner used to sit in, or go running to the door or window wagging their tail when no one is there. You might notice them staring intently at a spot or following something around the room when nothing is there.

Pets are very aware of otherworldly visitors, and don't think there's anything strange about it. It's common for their deceased owners to come see them and check in on them. They might sense the souls of other animals who resided in the home as well, even if those pets never knew each other in life.

Animals are different from most people in that they don't fear death. That lack of fear, combined with a sixth sense, allows them to easily see and hear spirits.

One of the things I love about being a medium is that the more you know about the afterlife, the less you fear death. Animals are ahead of us because they're born with that knowing. Animals can do more than sense when a ghost is around. Have you noticed that pets or farm animals know when a storm is coming? People explain that phenomenon by saying it's got to do with smells or some other physical sign, but I think it's their intuition. It's the same thing that helps animals know when their owner is ill or in danger.

Peacefully Crossing the Rainbow Bridge

Talk about a sixth sense. I recently had to put our cat down. Alexa and I love Bengal cats because they're so beautiful and affectionate. We were heartbroken when one of ours was diagnosed with cancer. The vet did what he could, but the cancer was too aggressive. We spent as many good weeks with her as we could, but there came a point when she was clearly ready to go. She wasn't her happy self, and we could tell she was uncomfortable.

I know how intuitive pets are, and thought that as soon as we walked into the vet's office, she would know what was going to happen. I didn't know how she would react. Mind you, this was a cat that hated the vet and was completely afraid of even routine vet visits.

Alexa and I wrapped her in a blanket, and the vet led us to a special room where they euthanized pets. I was so afraid to walk through the door with her. I just didn't want her to freak out.

But I was totally surprised by what happened. Alexa and I walked in and put her on the table. Immediately she started purring. I hadn't heard that sound in days! She was licking us and rubbing up against us. It was as if she was reassuring us that she knew what was coming and she was ready.

The cancer had run in the cat's family. We had brought her and her brother home as kittens. He had passed of the same cancer a couple of years before, and I could feel his presence and knew she did, too. We knew he was there to help her transition.

After cuddling and loving her for a few minutes, the vet came in and we said our goodbyes, knowing we would meet again. She left this world at peace and purring as loud as ever.

As much as we were upset, it gave us comfort to know she was not afraid of the journey ahead of her.

IS THERE A DIFFERENCE
BETWEEN GHOSTS AND SPIRITS?

Ghosts and spirits are the same thing, but the living have two different ways to describe them, and here's why: A spirit is a soul who you're familiar with—your grandma, your dad, your pet. Ghosts are just souls you don't have a connection with.

They are the same, it's just your own perception that differentiates them.

If I tell someone, "Your dad is with you in your house," they like that idea. But that same person would feel like their house was haunted if I told them the old owner was still on the premises!

The thing you have to remember is that even though you perceive them differently, ghosts are not evil. You might feel them from time to time, but that doesn't mean they have bad intent. Just like your family members visit you in Spirit, ghosts visit places that were meaningful to them in this world. And that might be the home they lived in before you did. If you feel a presence in your home, it's a good idea to think back and determine who that might be. Once we know who the ghost is, it's no longer a ghost. It's a spirit.

When I was little, I saw strange spirits in my home. I described them to my mother, and she recognized family members. She showed me a photo album, and I recognized them as the spirits who had visited me—my great-grandfather, aunt, and a cousin on my mom's side. She told me about each one and made them real to me.

Some were people I didn't recognize, but I told my mom about them, and she reassured me they were just neighbors who had passed and meant no harm.

Watching the Store!

The same thing happened to my friend when she started a fashion boutique. She moved into her new space and noticed lights flickering and doors opening and closing with no explanation. When she told her landlord, he said, "Don't worry, that's just Tom the barber. He was at this location until his barbershop burned down. He likes to check on the place every so often."

After hearing the story, my friend was anxious to learn more. She researched the property and found a picture of Tom. She and her partner framed the photo and hung it in the back of the shop. Every night, whoever closed up the store asked Tom to watch over the place. He had turned from a ghost to a spirit partner!

It all goes to show that ghosts and spirits are defined by your perception.

MY MOTHER-IN-LAW COULDN'T STAND ME WHEN SHE WAS ALIVE; WILL SHE COME BACK AND HAUNT ME AFTER SHE DIES?

You can cross that worry off your list! The answer is no because she already haunted you enough in life. In fact, she's likely to look back and feel remorseful for the way she treated you. Souls gain a new perspective after their life review, and if they can, they try to make it up to the people they treated unkindly.

I once had a client who went through this very thing. She was never able to make her husband's mother happy. My client tried everything she could think of to find common ground—she learned her recipes, bought her gifts for Mother's Day and holidays, and visited regularly—but nothing worked. Her mother-in-law was so protective of her son, that no woman could ever be good enough for him!

When her mother-in-law was diagnosed with Alzheimer's, my client took care of her. She made up a room in her house, cooked for her, and took her to doctor's appointments and to the beauty salon to get her hair done. But the more she did for the old woman, the more negative and difficult she became. After three years, every day felt like torture. My client continued for her husband's sake, but she never got a bit of gratitude or kindness in return.

After her mother-in-law finally passed, the woman came for a reading. She expected to hear from her own mother, but wouldn't you know, her mother-in-law stepped to the front of the line.

She desperately wanted to give a long-overdue thank-you for all the love and support her daughter-in-law had given her, and she asked for forgiveness for how she behaved during her illness and even before it.

She wanted me to tell my client that now that she was in heaven, she considered the woman her daughter. She was so appreciative that despite everything, my client had cared for her as if she were her own mother. She made sure I encouraged my client to wear the jewelry that she had left behind.

This reading says it all. People who treated you badly in life are more interested in making amends than anything else. They gain clarity after they die, and they see the best in the people they left behind. They also can look back and see their own bad behavior without making excuses or getting defensive. Which leads me to our next question . . .

DO PEOPLE HAVE TO ANSWER FOR THEIR BAD DEEDS WHEN THEY DIE?

When a soul transitions, they look back on their time on earth as if they're watching a movie. Only from their new perspective, they can see the events very, very clearly. They review their entire life, the good and the bad. Some souls take longer than others to complete their review and progress to the next level. They might even have some tasks to do to help them raise their vibration.

It's kind of like AA in that way—you have to acknowledge what you've done and sometimes make amends to the people you've wronged before you can move on.

Making Amends

The life review shines a light on what really matters in life. When you're on the other side, you're no longer attached to your career, your bank balance, or your body-fat ratio. That's fine when you're alive, but you leave that stuff behind when you die. What you are left with is the love and compassion you shared, the people you helped, and the difference you made in the world.

You also see the unfinished business and the people you hurt. You see the results of the things you did *not* do, like the love you withheld and the time you didn't spend on things that mattered. You become fully aware of the ripple effect your behavior had on others. Luckily, it's never too late to make amends.

When a soul has completed their life review, the next step is to connect with the living and make things right.

I can think of many examples:

- A woman came to my event and immediately her mother came through and apologized for making her daughter feel so guilty for putting her in assisted living.

- A man came through and said that he wished that he could take back the vicious letter he had left for his wife, blaming her for his death. He was bipolar and had killed himself. Looking back, he realized that his problems had nothing to do with her.

- An older woman begged me to let her son know that she should never have pressured him to spend so much time with her and neglect his own children. She realized in her life review that she was being selfish.

The process of passing over, letting go of negative emotions, and looking back on their life is a gift that allows the soul to evolve. They have the opportunity to let go of any grudges or negative feelings, go through their life review, and then, when the time is right, help their loved ones on earth to learn from their experience and feel their love.

Forgiveness from Heaven

As a medium, I never know who will come through and try to talk to me. I will say that I find the best readings happen when someone shows up that you're not expecting to hear from. Because of the life review, sometimes souls that you barely knew will come through.

For example, I recently connected a woman with her father, whom she never got to know because he left home when she was just a child. Because of his selfish ways, she didn't even know he had died until years later.

After he passed, he was able to see the hurt and pain he caused his daughter by being absent from her life. He needed to get a message to her and explain his actions. He wanted her to know that he took full responsibility for his choices and that he was sorry. Because of this message, she could finally think of her dad and smile. In an instant, the years of pain just lifted away, and she could breathe again.

IF YOU WERE ANGRY IN LIFE, WILL YOU STILL BE ANGRY IN HEAVEN?

You can live your whole life being responsible, working hard, and playing by the rules—and still carry anger and negativity. You haven't done anything wrong, so it seems like there'd be no problem transitioning to heaven. On the other hand, it's hard to picture heaven being filled with cranky, resentful souls!

You've heard the term "You can't take it with you!" That applies to money, but also to anger, resentment, jealousy, and all the other heavy emotions that weigh people down in life.

But don't worry! The universe has everything under control. Here's how: imagine your personality traits and feelings are like grains of sand. Positive emotions like love, compassion, and kindness are like the finest, softest sand. On the other hand, anger, resentment, and jealousy are rough and heavy, like small stones. When a soul transitions to the other side, it's like passing through a sieve. The heavy emotions are filtered out, and only the light is allowed to pass through.

So if your good-hearted but irritable grandmother passes, a medium might still pick up on some of those traits because of the memories she reveals, but her actual soul being will be pure light.

IS THERE SUCH A THING AS PSYCHIC PROTECTION?

My mom always says that it's not ghosts and spirits you have to worry about, it's the living! Narcissists, people who take out their own insecurities and anger on others, or overly judgmental people can all drain your precious energy.

We call these individuals *energy vampires*.

What Are Energy Vampires?

Have you ever known someone who sucked the life out of you, leaving you exhausted and depleted?

Energy vampires can take the form of a family member, co-worker, or friend. When you're around that person, they turn your mood around.

Normally, energy vampires don't even know what they're doing. They're just selfish and stuck in the gear of negativity to the extent that it drags down other people.

Just like garlic wards off the vampires, there are secret protection techniques you can use to ward off psychic vampires.

The main people I help with psychic protection are my celebrity clients. Many people in the public eye feel depleted because of the scrutiny and rumors and jealousy pointed at them every day. From an energetic perspective, it's like an avalanche of negativity coming at them from the press and strangers. Social media makes the whole situation worse.

Fortunately, there are simple techniques that can deflect those waves of negativity.

Reflect Negativity Away with a "Circle of Mirrors"

Refusing to let the energy of others chip away at your own sense of well-being is pretty simple. Here's one exercise I share with my clients:

Focus on picturing a circle of outward-facing mirrors surrounding you. You can do it anytime you need to bounce toxic energy away from you. The mirrors only block out negative energy; all the positive stays with you on the opposite side of the mirror.

Out with the Bad, In with the Good!

I once had a client who was really struggling with her job. She had lost her confidence, due in part to a co-worker who would take every opportunity to belittle and berate her. It got to the point where she dreaded going to work. She came to me for a reading because she wanted to switch jobs, but she wanted to be sure she was making the right decision.

Spirit told her not to alter her life course and change jobs because of this person. She was liked by everyone else and was a valued member of the team. The person was jealous of the positive attention my client was getting. She hadn't even realized that she was so valued, because she was so focused on the negativity.

Spirit's advice was not to let the negativity have power over her, and to rise above it. By using psychic protection, she was able to send the negativity back to the person sending it, and let in the positive. Over a few weeks, she realized that she wasn't bothered by the snide, passive-aggressive comments. She was able to focus on her work and the contribution she was making.

Ironically enough, after a few months of her using psychic protection, that negative energy had nowhere to go, the destructive co-worker wound up leaving the job, and my client actually received a promotion.

WHY ARE OUIJA BOARDS BAD?

Remember when I said earlier that evil spirits won't bother you if you don't go looking for them? Well, Ouija boards are the definition of "looking for trouble." My mom and my grandma have always told me to avoid these at all costs!

As we discussed, there are both good and bad spirits. People go to Ouija boards to connect with Spirit, but using one opens up a portal to invite any spirit into your space—good or bad.

It's like protecting your house, in the same way you wouldn't go to bed with your doors unlocked, you don't want to leave your space open to just any spirits. You want to have complete control over whom you talk to.

Before I was practicing I once had a co-worker in Boston who was so freaked out because her daughter had been playing with a Ouija board with friends. The girl hadn't touched the board herself but was in the room when it was being used. Even though she tried to steer clear, there were messages on the board that were directed to her. She told her mom and was completely freaked out. She had begged her friends to stop, but they didn't listen. She asked her mom to ask me, because she was afraid she had carried something home.

It turned out she was safe. There had been a negative soul trying to reach out to her. Because she kept rejecting it, she was able to walk away without harm—but that was a *very* close encounter. She didn't realize how lucky she was. Had she engaged with it, she could have allowed that spirit into her home.

If you use a Ouija board, it's hard to undo the damage. Even though you put it away—or even get rid of it, the harm is done. Using the board invites the spirits in, but getting rid of it doesn't get rid of them.

If you don't want to run a bed and breakfast for spirits, it's best to leave the Ouija boards alone.

The reason you never see psychics and mediums using them is that there's no reason to, and they don't want to put their communication line at risk by letting in negative souls.

Now, don't get me wrong. There are people I know who have used these boards and nothing bad happened. That's probably because there wasn't a negative soul nearby. It's like not wearing a seat belt; you're fine as long as there's not a problem—but all it takes is one accident to make sure you use your seat belt every time.

Tarot cards and tea leaves are different. They provide a safe way for psychics and mediums to navigate their gift while using something physical and maintaining control. They don't summon spirits; they just help the psychic or medium made sense of the vision they are seeing. Tarot cards and tea leaves are used along with your psychic gift. They utilize your own psychic channel in connecting with the afterlife.

GOING DEEPER
Replacing Negative Thoughts
with Positive Energy

People always want to know how they can protect themselves from negative energy. My advice is to make sure to pay attention to the negativity you yourself might be sending out. Remember, you attract what you focus on. The more positive your thoughts are, the less of a window you open up for negativity.

When you focus on negativity, you give it life and energy. When you ignore it and instead focus on positive things, you take that energy away. Remember that you can set boundaries—you don't have to let negative energy become your energy. You are in control of your own life and happiness.

We all feel bad sometimes; and some situations, like the loss of a loved one, are hard to recover from. Instead of focusing on your feelings of sadness, accept them for what they are, but make it a point to experience a little joy every day.

FIND OUT HOW TO FEEL BETTER FAST
AND MAKE IT LAST

During tough and challenging times, it's important to remind yourself of the things about your life that are good, so you don't lose sight of what really matters!

NUMBER ONE: Never stop believing in yourself. Remember that heaven has a divine plan for you. You can call upon your angels, guides, and loved ones in spirit whenever you need divine assistance.

NUMBER TWO: Reach out to your family and friends for support. The people in our lives who truly care about us are there when we need them the most. There are some things in life that you are not meant to go through alone.

NUMBER THREE: Live one day at a time, focusing on today instead of worrying about yesterday or tomorrow. By living only in the present you can avoid stress, anxiety, and depression by staying focused on what's right in front of you instead of stressing about the unknown. A friend of mine once told me that 90 percent of the things we stress over never end up happening. So why stress?

NUMBER FOUR: Exercise and stretch. When I am feeling stressed or anxious, one of the best ways to deal with it is by exercising for at least fifteen minutes a day. For me, walking is my medicine. Not only does exercise release endorphins in our bodies—which make us feel better—but oftentimes when we are experiencing stress and anxiety, all we can think about is what made us upset. When you exercise, you reset your mind and reconnect with your soul.

NUMBER FIVE: Be grateful every day. This probably goes without saying, but it is so important to stay positive through tough times. Being grateful for what you have, no matter how big or small, will give your life more meaning and make you feel better about yourself. You can do this by ending each night with a gratitude list.

USE NATURE AS YOUR SIGNAL
TO RELEASE SADNESS AND STRESS

One of the best ways to heal anxious thoughts and anxiety is by spending time appreciating nature. When you remove yourself from your daily surroundings, you find peace and tranquility. Nature helps to relieve your mind of its worries with its pureness.

Start by finding a place where you feel comfortable walking. I recommend finding a space a little distance from home—a new space that can be your safe haven for releasing stress and anxiety. A place where every time you visit it, you can leave your thoughts, worries, and anxieties behind.

When you are feeling the burdens of stress and worry, visit this place alone.

This is a safe place. When you are there, you are free to think through all the thoughts and worries that are bothering you.

While you're there, try to take the focus of your thoughts from being kept inward, to being released outward so they will no longer weigh you down. Imagine your negative thoughts as balloons and release them up into the sky.

In life we tend to bury our thoughts and let them add up without addressing them. Doing this for any amount of time can usually cause them to feel overwhelming. While you're in your safe, natural place, you can make the decision to leave your sadness and worry behind and stay in the present moment. Take a break from the anxious thoughts and focus on nature. Look at the birds, animals, and breathe the smells. Just give yourself time to relax.

PROTECTION EXERCISES

Even though 99 percent of the negativity we encounter is not coming from demons or darkness, there might be a time you encounter something you can't explain. Even though dark spirits can't hurt you when your own energy is positive, there are a few things you can do to give yourself a little extra protection. And like my mom always says, the only people you have to fear are the living. Well, these techniques help with those earthly encounters, too.

- Imagine a mirrored wall around you, forming a wall and reflecting negative energy away from you.

- Get to know your angels and guides and call upon them to protect you.

- Clear stagnant energy out of any living space that feels uncomfortable to you by burning sage. It really works!

- Take a few steps to infuse spaces that are new to you with your own energy. I like to personalize hotel rooms by putting a photo of Alexa and our two cats on the nightstand, and by playing some of my favorite disco tunes.

- When all else fails, open the windows and let the sunshine and fresh air in.

CHAPTER 9

Heal, Manifest, and Transform Your Life

*"We are born with a life purpose—
and we are meant to fulfill it."*

WHY ARE WE HERE ON EARTH?

First of all, even though I've always been called an old soul, I'm only thirty, and I wouldn't have a clue about the meaning of life except for the connection I have to souls on the other side. Some of these souls are very old, and every one of them has access to divine wisdom. So any insights about the meaning of life originate from them, but I'll do my best to explain to you what they've told me.

You may not agree with everything you read here—and that's fine. Just take away what touches your heart.

So here goes . . .

I like to consider that the earth is a classroom. It's here that we learn our life lessons, meet our soul mate, find our purpose, and adopt our pets. Also, we make connections that we carry with us to the other side.

Think of it this way. The physical world and the spiritual world are not separate. If they were, I wouldn't be able to connect to heaven while I'm alive. But heaven and earth, and every being living or dead, is connected. And we are all here on earth to add to these connections as if we were helping to build an enormous web. Everything you create here carries over.

It's easy to get caught up in the day-to-day stuff, like cutting the lawn and paying taxes, but that's not the only reason you're here. The love and kindness and compassion you share with other people, animals, even plants and nature have a profound impact here and on the other side.

When something comes up in a reading about a dispute, or family members who are not speaking, Spirit always tells me the same thing. While we're here on this earth, we only have each other. That's why it's important to be kind to each other.

And as far as the web or connection, know that one generation affects the next. No one is in a vacuum. And if you're wondering about different religions all being connected to heaven and to each other, there are countless ways to connect. No one is excluded.

This is already starting to be a really complicated question, so I've broken it down into different questions and answers, following.

WHY DO WE FACE CHALLENGES AND STRUGGLES IN OUR LIFE?

I've learned personally, and from Spirit, that every struggle is there to teach us a lesson.

If you're having a hard time, know that you're not alone. Even those people who seem like they have the perfect life are dealing with struggles. They may have health issues, addiction, mental illness, relationship problems, career struggles. If they didn't, they wouldn't experience growth in this lifetime.

So don't feel cheated if you have obstacles and problems in your life. The satisfaction and learning come from overcoming them and becoming your own success story. Our challenges and struggles shape who we are, and they have a profound impact on the people who hear our stories. We can create a positive ripple effect just by telling our stories, and at an even simpler level, just by the way we treat others.

How My High School Years Shaped the Person I Am Today

I promise you, anyone who meets me today wouldn't have recognized me in high school. I didn't talk much, I ate lunch alone, and my deepest wish was just to blend into the background and disappear. I felt as if no one understood me.

That insecure teenager was not a reflection of who I really was! But I was afraid to be myself—and afraid to be seen. I had a reaction to medication that caused severe acne, plus I didn't have a way to connect with the other kids. I was from Rhode Island, going to a school in Boston, and I couldn't relate to the kids there. I didn't like sports and I had a heavy Rhode Island accent. (It's not like people don't speak with an accent in Boston, but mine stood out.) People would make fun of me and tease me.

I begged my parents to let me change schools, and they finally agreed. Things got better for a little while. But then I started sharing my gift. Being in the limelight had its challenges, because the bullying started all over again. I was about nineteen years old, and still connected to my old high school friends. Unfortunately, those friends didn't understand my gift, and I was getting teased—even getting prank calls. People I barely knew were making fun of me.

But I'd grown up a little, and I had made the decision to stop hiding who I was—to tune out the noise and to work on my mediumship. I gained confidence traveling my own path and I cut ties with the negative people in my life. But as much as some people were still negative, my true friends started to show themselves.

Things Got Better . . .

As I got more comfortable with letting the "real Matt" emerge, I started attracting new friends and new opportunities. As I gained more notoriety in my hometown, the people whom I had cut out of my life started reaching out, but I was busy with my new friends and career. I was polite to them, but they'd already demonstrated who they were. That ship had already sailed!

The whole experience was so eye-opening. I realized that once you cut that negative energy out of your life, you create a new pathway. I went from being afraid to talk, to being my loud and crazy self. And not only did I find people who were like me and appreciated exactly who I was, but I got the chance to reach out to a whole new community through my television appearances, live and virtual events, even my books!

My adult self is nothing like that scared kid hiding out in the cafeteria. I would never have experienced the amazing life I have now if I hadn't broken through my fear.

Being myself was one important lesson I had to learn, and it was life-changing. Not only did things get better for me personally, but I gained insight and empathy for what other people were going through. And I think that was the biggest part of my own life lesson.

I'VE EXPERIENCED A LOSS. HOW WILL I GET OVER THIS PAIN AND GRIEF?

Losing a loved one is the hardest thing you can go through, but let me tell you, you will get through it. Every day I see people heal and release their pain.

The tough part about grief is how it's different for everyone. There are stages of grief, but everybody experiences them to different degrees, even in different order. And everyone heals in their own way.

Getting Past the Initial Shock, and Starting to Heal

Don't let anyone make you feel that there is a particular process or schedule for grief. Dealing with loss is your own personal journey, and what works for someone else might not work for you. But it's also important to know the difference between the initial shock and pain of loss, and healing pain.

When you lose a loved one, you might feel hopeless and like you can't go on. You might have the urge to hide out and not face the memories. You can do that, but there's a point where you need to start doing things that may hurt, but that will also heal.

For example, going through old photos is painful, but the process is healing. Clearing out your loved one's old clothes and donating them to someone in need can be hard, but it's also healing.

One of the things that can help you recover from grief and pain is exploring just where your pain is coming from. One way to do that is by taking a personal inventory.

Ask yourself the following questions. Really think about them and be sure you're answering based on your actual feelings. There are no "right" answers.

GRIEF INVENTORY:

1. I should have [actions not taken before their death].

2. I'm a bad person if I don't think about [loved one] all the time.

3. I'm a bad person if I move on.

4. I should have been a better [role in that relationship].

5. I shouldn't dishonor the memory of [loved one] by talking or thinking about their shortcomings.

Thinking through your answers will help you come to terms with your feelings. When you pinpoint the places where you're stuck, you might want to discuss them with a trusted friend or a therapist. I promise, it may hurt, but it will ultimately help you heal. Healing pain is like getting a massage. It hurts to get the knots worked out, but you feel better after.

Unpacking Memories

Your loved one doesn't want to see you stuck, and they'll try to push you to move on. This story illustrates that. I met a woman at one of my events. She looked familiar because she'd attended several group events, hoping to connect with her daughter, but the girl had never come through.

Finally, at her fourth event, I was drawn to the bereaved mother. I could see that her daughter was behind her in Spirit. The young woman had passed from cancer. Her family had done everything they could. They were convinced she could beat it, but the cancer was too aggressive. It broke her mother's heart when she passed.

The girl showed me a room filled with boxes and told me they had been at her mother's home for fifteen years. The girl indicated that seeing them was causing her mother pain. When I told her this, the woman started crying. She was so afraid of the pain she would feel if she opened the boxes filled with her daughter's belongings. She didn't want to relive the memories by going through the boxes. But what was happening was that her daughter's memory was fading away.

The daughter was insistent. *"You've told yourself for fifteen years that you're not ready but it's time!"* The girl wouldn't let her mother off the hook. She wanted her mother to promise to go through the boxes. *"There are things in those boxes she needs to see—happy memories that will help her heal."*

The woman promised, and I wondered if she would follow through.

I found out when the woman came back for another event. This time she had her family with her, and her whole energy had changed. She had color in her cheeks and was dressed nicely in a colorful blouse. She had a smile on her face!

"You changed my whole life! At first it was so hard, but as I started going through the boxes, my pain got less, and my memories of my daughter returned."

I would have liked to have taken credit, but I had to tell her, "I didn't change your life—your daughter did."

Helping Someone Navigate Grief

Grief can make you question so many things and can change you as a person. But the more you choose to keep your loved one's memory alive, the more connected you feel to Spirit—and that in itself is a blessing.

I'm always so honored to be able to help a grieving person to heal. But you don't have to be a medium to do that. If you know someone who is grieving, don't be afraid to mention their loved one. Even better, tell a story that will bring that person to life.

A special note for parents: it's so heartbreaking when your child passes at any age, but know that they are always going to be connected to you. Parents who have lost a child dread the question, "How many children do you have?" Say their name, and don't be afraid. Don't make them disappear because you don't want to explain.

I wish I could give everyone a chance to see loss through my eyes, and to see how the people you miss are actually watching over you, wishing you happiness and healing.

HOW CAN I GET A MESSAGE TO MY LOVED ONE?

People ask me all the time, "Matt, can you tell my loved one how much I love them?" I tell them it doesn't work that way. As a medium, I deliver messages from heaven, but you don't need me to talk to someone who has passed. You can connect with them at any time.

Your loved one is literally just a thought away. The moment a loved one in heaven comes to mind, picture yourself ringing a doorbell or sending a text. The minute you think about them, they are alerted.

But there are other ways to send a message:

• You can say a message out loud

• Have a conversation with them in your head

• Write it down on a piece of paper

Whatever way you choose to reach out, they will get the message and know it's from you.

Wait! What Do I Say?

I remember when my grandmother was alive, she loved talking to me. It didn't matter what I was telling her, she just loved the connection. It's the same now that she is in heaven. Your loved one loves hearing from you as much as you enjoy hearing from them. You can tell them just about anything:

- Tell them about your day

- Let them know what family members are up to

- Ask for their help: "Mom, I have a job interview, please help me with my anxiety."

Don't overthink things. The same things you'd talk about when you were both in this world can be communicated to them when they pass. If you loved telling your mom funny stories about the kids, or asking your dad for advice, don't stop when they pass.

Visiting the Grave Site

People make a big point of going to the grave of a loved one, but to be honest, that's more comforting for the living person. The dead person doesn't care where you are, just that you're thinking of them.

The person you're talking to isn't in the ground, and you can talk to them anywhere—in the car, in the shower, when you walk the dog.

I was doing a reading, and the woman kept thinking, *I hope my mom doesn't know about Billy!* I asked her, "Who is Billy?"

"How did you know? Are you reading my mind?"

"No, your mom told me! She can hear your thoughts."

It turns out Billy was an old flame whom her mom hadn't liked, and they were dating again. She didn't want her mother to know, but you can't keep things from someone who has passed, and you don't have to!

Your loved ones in heaven aren't judging you, although they might see the situation for what it is and gently steer you in the right direction.

As a medium, I've seen people send messages to their loved ones in many ways—balloons, paper lanterns, even texting their cell phone after they died . . . which leads to my next story.

This Number Is No Longer in Service . . .

I was doing a reading for a young girl who had lost her dad. After he passed, every night she called his phone, listened to his voice, and left a message. It helped her feel connected to him. One night she called and was heartbroken when she found that the number was disconnected.

Her father came through and told her, *"The phone may be disconnected, but there is no disconnect between us! I received all your messages, but you don't need my old cell phone number. You can call me anytime."*

WHY DO CERTAIN PEOPLE COME INTO OUR LIVES ONLY TO HURT US OR LET US DOWN?

Life is a constant journey. There are people who are with us for our entire lifetime (and beyond), and others who are just with us part of the way.

Sometimes when relationships go bad, we question why those people were ever in our lives at all.

Recently a friend came to me very upset. She had a close friend whom she'd met when they worked at a big law firm. They decided to break out on their own, and for twenty-five years they had a successful law practice together. They were so focused on building the business as a team that they could not imagine ever going their separate ways. For twenty-five years they helped clients, changed lives, and built a strong reputation in the community.

Then, one day, things changed. One of the business partners decided she no longer wanted to work so hard and that it was time to retire. The other partner wasn't prepared for this and tried to talk her partner out of leaving. Despite trying to make it work, the building was put up for sale and one party was forced to buy the other out. In the end, the business wasn't the only thing that was dissolved. The friendship was too.

My friend asked me, "Why did this person even come into my life if they were going to end up being so self-centered!" I encouraged her to look at it from a different perspective. In reality, if they hadn't met each other, they would never have been able to build such a successful business that was rewarding for them, and that had helped the community for twenty-five wonderful years.

Now, there wasn't a death in this instance—but losing a business, job, or friendship is a loss too. And just like when you think of someone who's passed, it's important to remember the events of their whole life, not just the passing.

You're on your own journey. Regardless of the people who come and go, and all the crazy things that happen along the way, heaven will always work to help keep you on your own path.

Life happens, and people exercise their free will. But other people are in our lives up to a certain point, to help us discover things about ourselves.

One bit of wisdom I've heard from the souls I've connected with is to not take things so personally. Most people aren't trying to hurt you; they are on their own journey.

No matter what happens and how many people come into your life, it's important to keep an open heart. Even if your relationships change, don't close the door on the memories. You can keep in touch. Even if relationships change, at least look back over the relationship and try to remember the positive aspects, and what they taught you.

WHY AM I HERE? HOW CAN I DISCOVER MY TRUE PURPOSE?

Finding your purpose is not so much about finding the meaning of *your* life but about learning how to make the best use of your gifts and talents. But if I had a dollar for every person who asked me if I could help them identify their unique gifts, well, I'd have a lot of cash!

Uncovering Your Gifts, and Figuring Out How to Use Them

Some people are painters, some are musicians. Some are natural teachers, inventors, healers, and leaders. Where do you fit in? If you don't fit into an established career, maybe your calling is to start a brand-new path and inspire positive change in the world.

It's not just about your career, it's about living your dream and sharing what you have in your heart.

If you can't identify your calling, I have one thing to tell you: Don't overthink it! Just look back to what you love. What are you really good at and what do you enjoy doing most? If you're browsing through a series of articles on your phone or computer, what do you click on?

Think about the struggles and challenges that you have gone through in your life. How could you use those skills to help someone going through the same or something similar?

Also think about times when you're totally in the zone. You can tell when you're there, because time disappears, and you become completely absorbed in what you are doing.

You've Figured Out Your Purpose—Now What?

So many people encounter opportunities but are afraid to take the first step. If you are open and aware, the universe will often lend you a hand.

A good friend of mine in Boston loves kids. She always wanted to be a teacher, but her life took her in a different direction and she became an administrative assistant. Even though it wasn't her true calling, she was good at her job, and the people she worked with trusted and respected her. But each day she noticed something. Many of the executives in her firm were struggling with a problem. They had a busy schedule of meetings, business travel and dinners, and there was often no one to watch their kids. Seeing that they needed help, she offered to babysit for a few of them. After helping them out, it became a regular part of her week. More and more people at work started asking her for help after hours, and she found herself booked solid!

That gave my friend an idea. "What if I open up a babysitting center in the city for moms and dads who need help?" She started talking to other people she knew who also loved kids, and she started a child-sitting service. It took off! More and more people found out about her service, and there was an endless supply of people looking for sitters. Looking back, she realized that she had never deviated from her path; instead, her job as an administrative assistant helped her gain the trust of the right group of people, which led her to a new career.

Remember the connections that I talked about building? This is a great example of how that works. She connected her administrative assistant skills with people who had a need, and then connected that with people who also had the same dream, for the perfect career. And she not only became very successful financially, but she was providing a valuable service for others.

THE LAW OF ATTRACTION SEEMS TOO GOOD TO BE TRUE! IS IT REAL?

It's totally real! Remember that we're all energy. And as an energetic being, you're like a big magnet. Every thought, action, and word you send out attracts more of the same to you.

People love to think that success is all about luck and having the inside track somehow. But if you focus on the fact that you don't have that kind of luck, guess what? You won't attract opportunities. The law of attraction works both ways. Negative thoughts attract more negativity. Positive thoughts attract positive things.

We all have the gift to create the life we want. We were born with a road map in our hands and if we stay mindful and positive, the universe will nudge us and keep us on course.

Here's a story from my own life to illustrate my point. Remember that vision board I was telling you about earlier? Well, here is how it all took place. . . .

I was in a long relationship, and while she was a great person and we had fun together, I think we both knew we were not soul mates.

When that relationship ended, I knew I was ready to find my one and only. Now, years before, I'd judged the Miss America pageant and I was so impressed with the women I met. Not only were they beautiful and stylish, but they were smart and caring and used their platform to make a difference. I thought, *Imagine being with someone like that.*

I knew the law of attraction worked, so I created a vision board. I put on it everything I wanted in a partner. I could visualize her in my mind, and I put it all on the vision board—a pageant girl, with dark hair and eyes, living in Rhode Island.

A little after that, I was doing an event at a center, and backstage I ran into the producer of the Miss Massachusetts pageant that was going on at the same time. She invited me to come next door to meet the women.

While I was talking to them, a woman came up who recognized me from my television appearances. We got to talking, and she asked if I was seeing anyone. She said, "I have the perfect woman for you! She was Miss Rhode Island." *Oh wow! My vision board is working.* I was so excited! But no, she was a nice girl; it just wasn't a hit. This was weird! I found the girl on my vision board, but there was no chemistry.

Then one night I was scrolling through Instagram and noticed a beautiful girl who had just started following me. It said that she was Miss Rhode Island. How could this be? I thought I'd met her! Turned out the girl I had met was a past winner, and Alexa was the current Miss Rhode Island.

I didn't waste any time. I messaged her and we met for coffee, and from that moment on, it just flowed! I realized everything that had happened in my relationships up to then was just leading me to meeting Alexa, and now we're married.

HOW DO I MAKE THE LAW OF ATTRACTION WORK FOR ME?

Have you ever asked a mentor or someone in a position you aspire to at work for advice about getting a promotion? They'll tell you to dress and behave as if you're already in the job. Some people slack off a little or don't act as professionally as they could, and tell themselves that they'll improve once they get promoted. Then they wonder why that promotion never comes. The secret of getting what you want at work, and in life, is actually pretty simple.

Five Steps to Start Manifesting Happiness

STEP ONE: LET ANY NEGATIVITY THAT CAUSED YOU STRESS IN PAST YEARS STAY THERE

Negativity can drain you and make you feel like you are sinking, but only if you let it! When you say enough is enough, and make the decision to release the pressure and heaviness that you have been feeling, it can no longer control you. Leave the negativity behind and decide that whatever was on your mind and caused you to feel stressed will no longer be able to enter into your life. Instead, focus on inviting in the new—replace every negative thought or challenge with something or someone more positive who will bring you joy and complement your life.

STEP TWO: SURROUND YOURSELF WITH FAMILY AND FRIENDS WHO BRING YOU HAPPINESS

Is there someone you have been meaning to contact or reconnect with, but you keep putting it off? Make them part of your life by giving them a call and reconnecting. The people who you reach out to now will remain connected to you throughout the next year. If nobody comes to mind who you want to reconnect with, focus on creating relationships and bringing new friends into your life. Life is so much more fun when you have people around you with whom you can make memories and enjoy life. It can feel uncomfortable at first to step out of your comfort zone and meet new people, but when you do, you will love the experiences and friends you make and enjoy along the way.

STEP THREE: SET THE GOALS YOU WANT TO ACHIEVE (SERIOUS ONES THIS TIME)

I know that in the past you may have set a goal and not had the opportunity to complete it. This year you're not going to let that happen. To ensure that you stick to your goal and manifest it, take out your calendar and write in your goal every week. This works best if you write your goal in the beginning of the week, such as on Monday. Now your goal is part of your daily schedule, and you will be reminded each week to work toward it. At the end of the week, write down what steps you took toward accomplishing your goal. At the end of the year, when you look back at your calendar, you will see all of the progress that you have made. Pretty cool, right?

STEP FOUR: NEVER TAKE NO AS AN ANSWER

A roadblock might be in your path, but that does not mean you need to slow down. You can accomplish anything that you set your mind to. Know that heaven has created a plan for you to follow, and this plan will lead you to success if you're willing to take steps too. If something does not work out right away, do not give up, because the timing may just be off. Instead, take a moment to pause, look around you, and pursue another opportunity. Some things in life fall apart so that others can fall together in a better way. Just because the answer is no doesn't mean that there is not a better opportunity waiting for you to discover. Heaven will always lead you to the path that will benefit your highest and best good. Trust where this path is leading you.

STEP FIVE: IT'S OKAY TO PUT YOURSELF FIRST ONCE IN A WHILE

How many times have you said that you wish you had just one day to yourself, when you didn't have to worry about anyone else? Make that a reality this year by planning one day a month to take a personal day for yourself. On this day don't do anything that involves work, bills, or chores. Instead, focus on just relaxing and freeing your mind from all the everyday stress that has been accumulating. You can do anything on this day that will help you to relax and get back in touch with your soul. Days like this will help you to recharge your energy, and help you to balance the overload that you have been feeling.

CAN POSITIVE THOUGHTS HEAL YOU?

I was an EMT before I became a psychic medium and I'm familiar with both traditional and holistic medicine and see the value of both. Taking that into account, I believe we heal from the inside out. It starts with our thoughts and feelings.

Happy Stories Produce Positive Results

In this day and age, there is a pill for everything. Whether you have a headache, anxiety, or can't sleep, there is a pill for you. But what else can you do to heal?

A few years ago, I was invited to attend an event called Imagination Heals. It was a program for sick children who were battling life-threatening illnesses. The program introduced positive books, movies, and audio CDs into hospitals where children were recovering or undergoing treatment.

The program used fictional characters who had challenges of their own and used positivity to overcome them. The hope was that while children were undergoing traditional medicine, they would also reach for and listen to these programs and relate to the characters and start to think positively. The results were amazing! The children started to respond to treatment and healed almost 80 percent faster than other kids. The doctors found that by keeping the children's minds off their treatments, they were able to heal more and more; plus, the children loved it!

Kids Just Want to Be Kids

I remember my first experience in Peru working with sick children at an infirmary, I was scared to walk in. I was only seventeen years old and didn't know what I would witness, but I sucked up my emotions, held it together, and walked through the door. I was immediately overwhelmed. Children had been burned in fires, were sick with cancer, had infections, etcetera. I couldn't help but feel bad. I looked over to one child who was wearing a face mask. He looked up at the hat on my head and started to laugh. I picked it up off my head and put it on his. He was giggling and laughing.

All the kids started running around us. Once I started playing with them, I didn't see them as sick children anymore. They were laughing, joking, and loving the attention. They were regular kids, but they were fighting their battles of illness. Their strength was amazing and inspiring. I later realized it was because they didn't view themselves as sick. They just wanted to be regular children and treated as normal.

Looking back on this, there is a very valuable lesson we can learn from them about healing. It's a journey of the mind, soul, and body. When you are sick, don't let life get you down. Choose to continue living your life, and don't let your illness control or hold power over you. Love and enjoy each day and try to get back to normal by letting your good days shine through the tough ones.

When you keep a positive mindset and believe in yourself, you begin to heal.

The Power of Positive Thinking

I had a great aunt who found out she had stage 4 breast cancer. It had metastasized to her lungs, and she had to have part of her lung and her lymph nodes removed. Afterward the whole family was shocked, because she was adamant that she was not going to have chemotherapy.

The doctor urged her to take advantage of every possible treatment because the cancer was so aggressive, but she wanted to do things her way.

She was looking for remedies, and she came across a tea called ESSIAC that was getting good results. Going against her doctor's advice, she decided to try an alternative therapy. She kept drinking her special tea, and each day she repeated positive affirmations, "I'm going into remission; my body is healthy; I'm going to heal."

Every day, while drinking her tea she would close her eyes and try a meditation technique.

She would imagine millions of tiny scrubbing bubbles going through her body, polishing away all the bad cells. She would tell the bubbles, "You know what to do!" Her journey was far from pleasant. It was painful, tough, and mentally and physically challenging. Of course there was fear, but she pushed her fears aside and had faith in her positive thinking.

Every time she went to the doctor, she got more good news. Despite the initial grim diagnosis, her body was healing. Her doctor went from believing she didn't have a chance, to looking at her results as a miracle.

She lived well into her old age without any recurrences.

Don't get me wrong, I believe that God works through the hands of doctors and nurses, but your own positivity is also a powerful tool to help your recovery.

DO PRAYERS WORK?

Yes, absolutely! Let's start by talking about praying for other people. Sending thoughts and prayers isn't just a platitude. I believe when you sincerely pray for someone, you send a piece of your own healing energy to be with that person. You can also bring in "reinforcements" by asking your angels to help that person as well.

The more prayers that come through, the better. I think of prayers being like bricks—they build on each other. Lately I've been seeing more commercials for places like St. Jude's hospital for children. In addition to helping with a donation, I make it a point to send a prayer every time I see the commercial—or anytime I think of those children. I hope everyone who is watching sends a prayer, because the positive energy will build up and I know it will help. You don't have to be at someone's bedside for prayers to work. The positive energy doesn't have boundaries!

Heavenly Love During COVID-19

I did a reading for a woman whose mom was in a home with Alzheimer's. Her daughter went to the nursing home almost every day to spend time with her mom, bring her food, and look through photo albums with her. When Covid hit, the nursing home shut down and no visitors were allowed in. The woman was worried because suddenly she couldn't be with her mom, or even send food. Because of her mom's condition, it wasn't even possible to call or FaceTime. All the woman was able to do was pray—and she did that every single night. She also asked her father, who had passed, to watch over her mom. Sure enough, the father came through in a reading and assured her he'd received her prayers and was watching over her mother.

Before every reading and event I say a silent prayer. I pray that the people who are grieving get the messages they need and connect with loved ones who can help them heal. I can feel the power of that simple prayer, and I know it helps!

GOING DEEPER
Understanding Life's Lessons

Think back on your life. How has the way you approach life changed as you've grown, been influenced by other people, had experiences, and traveled. Sometimes the most life-changing experiences are the ones that are tough to go through, but you come out better on the other side.

Myself, I realize that by being bullied in high school, I learned not only who I am but what kind of people I want to spend my time with as well. It also helped me to be compassionate when dealing with people who are struggling or grieving.

Sometimes you can look back on your life and see just the negative. "My parents divorced, my relationship ended, I was fired from my job, I struggled financially." While you can't deny that those challenges were there, you can reprogram your brain to see them differently. To do this, why not take a quick inventory of the people and events in your life that taught you the greatest lessons.

Sit quietly and try to calm your mind. Think back on your life. Revisit your childhood, your teens, your twenties, and so on. In every period, think about the events that stand out. Use your intuition to capture thoughts that pop into your head, even if they don't seem relevant. Jot down your insights.

When you have a good list of meaningful events and people, reflect on what they taught you. You might want to journal about them or have a conversation with a trusted friend. Really dig for the lessons. How did your divorce help you to grow stronger?

What did the death of a pet teach you about appreciating unconditional love? How did your critical mother or boss teach you about protecting your energy? By reviewing your past experiences, you'll be better able to identify new lessons and opportunities for growth.

CHAPTER 10

A Few Last Thoughts About Karma, Divine Guidance, Energy, and the Universe

*"The more you learn about heaven,
the more it becomes a familiar place."*

CAN SPIRITS BE AROUND MORE THAN ONE PERSON AT ONCE? HOW?

Yes. Understandably, a lot of people wonder exactly how this works. It's best not to overthink it and just accept the fact that spirits can be in more than one place and with more than one person at a time. Why? Because they are limitless. That's a hard concept to get our heads around because we're human. But think about a Skype or Zoom call. Most of us don't know exactly how the technology works, but you know you don't have to leave your house to be on a video call with a family member across the globe. Your loved one doesn't actually leave heaven to connect with you, just like you don't leave your office or living room to video chat with people in other places.

Sharing a Rainbow

This question reminds me of the day I was driving home and saw the most amazing rainbow over my house. I went inside and grabbed my family, and we all ran out to admire it. It was so big and bright, and it looked like it started in my backyard. I took a photo and posted it on Facebook. Ten minutes later I saw that dozens of people on my feed had posted the same rainbow arching over their own homes or across the freeway on their way to work! It felt like it was right over my house, but it was everywhere—just like heaven.

Many people get nervous when they hear that a loved one is watching over another family member and not them. They don't need to worry! In fact, if one person is feeling the presence, chances are others will feel that same soul's presence, too.

I've heard from Spirit that it's a great relief when they get to heaven and realize they don't have to split their time between loved ones. Just like my rainbow, they can watch over everyone, and everyone will feel that personal connection.

DO SPIRITS EAT AND GO TO THE BATHROOM?

This is actually a tricky one. There's not a yes or no answer, but maybe this story will help clarify.

I once did a reading for a family, and their grandpa came through. When he was alive, his evening ritual was to sit in his recliner and eat ice cream, and that's exactly what he showed me. The family was surprised: "Wait, people in heaven eat?"

People in heaven *can* eat, but they don't have to. They often come through doing the things they loved in life. It's not uncommon for me to see a chef cooking in the kitchen, or a father drinking a cup of coffee.

It's important to know that just because food comes up in a reading, it doesn't mean souls are eating three meals a day. They don't need food to survive (they're dead, after all), but they still take place in activities that represent their personalities and who they were in life.

Do I think that spirits might occasionally pour themselves a glass of wine and enjoy it with other souls? I know they do, but it's more of a symbolic thing than an actual meal or drink. Food and drinks have a whole different significance in heaven.

Enjoying What He Had Missed in Life

A family came to me whose father had passed. Before he died, he was having a terrible time with food. He was on a GI tube and couldn't stand the fact that he couldn't enjoy his favorite meals. He begged his family for a steak or a hamburger. They couldn't give it to him, and he suffered with those cravings for years until he passed.

When he came through in the reading, he was surrounded by food—steak, mashed potatoes, cheesecake—and he told me he'd gained back all the weight he had lost while he was ill. His family was so happy to see him back to his old self and enjoying the foods that he'd been denied when he was ill.

When a loved one passes away, they want you to remember them happy. This reading was very healing for the family and for the soul himself because it replaced the image they had of him being thin, hungry, and frustrated, with the image of his healthy, happy self in heaven surrounded by his favorite foods.

Overall, spirits don't need the same things that we do to survive, because survival isn't an issue anymore. There are no hospitals or cemeteries in heaven. If you see a family member jogging, showering, or eating a burger in heaven, that's just a way for them to come through to you.

What you're seeing isn't really your loved one eating. The earthly activity they're showing you is a link to their old self and the personality they still have in heaven.

This makes me think of Casper the Friendly Ghost! I loved that cartoon when I was a kid, and I remember when Casper's uncles were sitting at the table eating, and the was food going right through them. They didn't need the food, but they were still connected to the act of eating.

DO DEAD PEOPLE SLEEP IN HEAVEN?

This is the same as the last question, because the activities we need to stay healthy on earth don't apply in heaven. So the answer is no, and one of the reasons is that there is no day and night. There's no time at all. Heaven is infinite and limitless.

What's so amazing is that because Spirit is energy, when they go to the other side, they are infinite too. They don't need to rest, and they don't feel the effects of time.

That's the reason your loved ones can be with you anytime. If you call upon them, you can rest assured you won't be disturbing them while they're having dinner or sleeping.

It's almost like living in Alaska where it can be daytime or nighttime for days! Except in heaven, it's always daytime.

I can't help thinking of heaven as being like New York City or Vegas! There's never a time when everyone is inside or asleep. There are always people outside going about their business. The spirits don't even have an awareness of time.

Earthly Milestones Lose Their Meaning in Heaven

Milestones matter a lot to the living. Here on earth, we're defined by birth and death. We celebrate when a baby is born and mourn when someone passes. Time and dates are closely tracked in life, but they don't matter a bit in heaven.

Souls don't celebrate their own milestones in heaven, but they do celebrate important dates with you. Birthdays, anniversaries, and holidays draw them closer because they are attracted to family gatherings, love, and laughter.

IS MY LOVED ONE DIFFERENT IN HEAVEN?

The answer is yes, and no. Remember that during their transition into heaven, your loved ones only take the very best parts of them.

First they go through a life review and leave behind all the parts that are too "heavy" to carry into heaven. They are released from things like addiction, mental illness, and disabilities, but they hold on to the love they have for you. When they come through to a medium, they always want you to see and remember them at their best.

Souls in heaven are basically the most positive and authentic version of themselves. Imagine if you could make a Facebook page in heaven that best reflects your ideal self. There would be posts of you looking healthy and happy, enjoying your favorite activities, and having fun with loved ones.

Everyone's heavenly self is a little different, because it's still associated with who they were in life. Your heavenly self is like your most perfect Facebook profile picture. We all have that one picture of us that we feel we look so good in. It's the same way with your loved ones in heaven.

Despite all these differences between the living and dead, the one thing that endures across it all is their personality—and that's what makes my job so much fun! When I do a reading, I get to meet the soul's real self. If they were quirky in life, they're quirky when they come through to me. I can tell instantly if they're an introvert or an extrovert—funny or serious.

Has My Loved One Changed THAT Much?

Sometimes you might get a reading that doesn't add up. For example, a friend of mine just went to a pet psychic. She had a golden retriever who had passed. She was desperately wanting to connect with him because she missed him so much.

"Did your dog like to dress up? I'm seeing him holding a spear with a pitchfork and a Viking costume." My friend racked her brains to come up with a connection, but her dog never let her put so much as a tee shirt on him, much less a Viking costume!

We were together one day, and she told me the story. She had been obsessing over the reading—had her dog had a personality change?

I could tell that her dog hadn't changed, it was just a bad reading. You have to realize that there are readings that miss the mark, and it doesn't mean your loved one has changed, or is rooting for a different team!

Psychics are human, and they have different levels of ability, or they might just be having an off day.

If you were connected to a loved one and you knew who they were in life, think twice before you let a reading convince you that they've changed. A soul might say something that surprises you, and they are able to forgive and understand things differently, but their true self doesn't change when they pass.

WHAT ARE SPIRIT ORBS IN PICTURES?

People ask me if you can actually see spirits. The fact that they're energy makes them hard to see with the human eye. But you can see indications, traces, or signs of their presence. Have you ever taken a picture and later noticed a ball or spot of light? Spirit orbs are usually seen in photos but can sometimes be seen with the naked eye.

If a loved one is present when you're taking a photo, you might see a silhouette or shadow, but most commonly what shows up is an orb—a manifestation of their energy that the camera captures as they're passing by.

There are so many people who post pictures to my Facebook page, of holidays and celebrations, with orbs that they didn't notice. When they have time to review the photos, the orbs are there! It's no coincidence they show up during special occasions and gatherings. Spirit likes to be there when their loved ones are together.

Sometimes Spirit tells me they appear as orbs in photos, and the family has never even noticed. But after the reading, they look back over the photos and can see them!

When people show me orb photos, they expect me to be able to tell them exactly who the orb represents. Honestly, I can't read a lot into the orb photos; I don't have that gift. My mom has the gift of seeing who the orb represents.

I do remember one time when a woman came to me for a reading. She had just had a baby, and when she watched the baby on the video monitor, she could see an orb circling him!

The orb would hover over the baby every night, and the mother was a little freaked out! I watched the video and knew she had nothing to worry about. I could feel the loving presence of the woman's mother, and we realized that the orb showed up for the first time on the anniversary of her mother's death.

When you see an orb in a photo, think about when it was taken. Chances are it's a holiday, anniversary, or some other significant date.

HOW CAN I CALL UPON MY ANGELS FOR HELP?

Just send out a thought to your angels, and they'll be there! They love to help when you need guidance, protection, or a heavenly shoulder to lean on.

There are specific angels and even saints that can be called upon to help with different things.

One saint I call upon is St. Anthony, the saint of lost things. Like all angels and saints, St. Anthony doesn't just show up and hand you your lost car keys. Angels will not interfere with your life without permission unless you are in very serious danger, but they are always happy to help. All they need is an invitation from you. It doesn't have to be anything complicated. "Please help me," or, "Please help my loved one" will do just fine! And you don't even need to say it aloud—your angels will hear your thoughts and understand your intentions.

If you're missing a document, a ring, or you can't find your car in the parking lot, you can summon St. Anthony with this prayer. It doesn't matter if you're not Catholic—St. Anthony can help anyone from any faith!

"St. Anthony, St. Anthony, please look around: my (insert whatever you're looking for here) is lost and cannot be found."

I have a funny story. A couple of years ago, Alexa was cooking Thanksgiving dinner. The house was hot from all the cooking, so Alexa propped a window open. We didn't happen to see the cat slip out through the window, and we didn't notice he was gone until that night, when I had a vision that the cat had escaped. We looked and looked, but it wasn't till I said the St. Anthony prayer that the cat was found. As soon as I said the prayer, I saw an image of the cat in a neighbor's yard. Sure enough, that's where he was. I credit finding him to St. Anthony!

In my family, we say that when you pray to a saint, you invite them into your life. Any saint who wants to be around me is welcome, and I'll do anything to encourage them to stay near me. I have a St. Christopher medal in my car because he's the patron saint of travel. When Covid hit, I gave my family St. Rocco medals, because he is the saint of infectious diseases.

Having a saint in your life is comforting, and can also provide very real help and guidance when you need it.

DO MY LOVED ONES KNOW THAT I VISIT THEIR GRAVE?

Yes, absolutely, and it's not because they're hanging around the cemetery! It's you they're attracted to, and they can feel that you've taken the time to visit their grave and think of them.

Sometimes people put a lot of effort into visiting and maintaining grave sites. No matter what your loved one told you before they died, once they cross over, they care about *you*, not the place where the body they no longer occupy is buried.

I had a mother who came through in spirit. When she knew she was dying, she told her daughter that it was very important that she keep up her grave. She wanted fresh flowers changed regularly, and the grave kept up. She wanted people passing by her grave to know she was loved. The daughter maintained the grave for years, but eventually moved and wasn't able to visit the grave regularly. The mother said she knew the daughter wasn't visiting her grave anymore.

You should have seen her daughter's face! She was so nervous, thinking she was busted. But the mother said not to worry! From her new perspective, she realized it wasn't the grave that was important—it was having her daughter think of her lovingly and honor her memory.

People often ask me if I'm overwhelmed with messages when I go to a graveyard. Not at all! Spirits don't hang out at graveyards. I feel the residual emotion from the funerals, and I pick up on the energy from the living who visit the graves, but I don't get any more spirit connections there than I do anywhere else.

People put a lot of energy and money into choosing headstones or creating memorials like benches or plaques. These are a beautiful way to show your love, but they matter more to the living than they do to the dead, although they do appreciate your loving gesture.

If you put up a bench for your loved one, they're not sitting on it all the time in spirit. But if you go there and think of them, they will sit down with you.

It kind of makes sense if you think about it. For example, there's an organization I belong to, where if you donate money, they will put a brick on a walkway. We donated, and it's so cool to see the brick that reads DONATED BY THE FRASER FAMILY. I like seeing it when I pass by, but we don't just hang out by our brick!

Nothing Matters More Than Your Loving Thoughts

People have all kinds of ways of remembering their loved ones. One woman I met at an event was missing her brother, so she got the idea of sitting at his grave site and drinking a beer with him. He came through to me in a reading and told her he had been there with her!

Go to a cemetery or sit on your loved one's grave if that makes you feel better. But if you move away or you can't get there for some reason, it's okay. Just thinking about them is enough. It's the thought that counts! Creating a spot of remembrance in your home or garden serves the same purpose.

CAN PEOPLE DIE ALL OVER AGAIN IN HEAVEN?

Believe it or not, people ask this question. The answer is no, however, sometimes spirits decide to come back to earth again if they're fulfilling a divine job or a divine role. When they leave, they don't die again, they just assume their heavenly form.

Remember that your spirit is meant to live on—it's the part of you that never dies, and just like energy it's infinite. That being said, people in heaven don't take death as seriously as we do. To them, it's simply a transition.

In the lifetime of your soul, the years when you're alive are the shortest part. Once souls get to heaven, they don't even think of people as dying young, or living to a ripe old age—to them, the earthly part of life is always just a blip in the infinite lifetime of the soul.

IS KARMA REAL?

Yes, karma is real, and I have news for you—there is both good and bad karma. People often think of karma as a bad thing. People might even fear karma. But it goes both ways.

Bad karma always comes back on the giver. Good karma also comes back—which is important to remember. People get upset when they're good to someone or help them out and the person doesn't appreciate it. But you don't have to worry! The universe keeps track.

We all have a good karma "piggy bank" that stores up good karma for when we need it.

The universe has a way of keeping track, and every kind act adds up like money in the bank. When you have a time in your life when you need positive loving energy, that good fortune is there for you.

Planting Seeds of Kindness

I have a friend who's the epitome of good karma. She is always practicing gratitude, can be counted on to come through when a friend needs help, and is great at listening and giving advice. Even though her friends come and go, and some people don't appreciate her kindness and generosity, she never lets it get to her. She just keeps on being the kind, giving person she is.

She's been like this for as long as I've known her, but a few years back her life took a tumble. She was diagnosed with a very rare cancer that was considered to be virtually untreatable. Her doctors advised her to move to New York to see a specialist. The New York doctor had successfully treated others with the same illness, and she knew this was her only chance of survival. She had no idea how she would be able to afford the treatment and care, and barely had the energy to think about packing her things and moving!

She was never the type to ask for anything, but a friend secretly created a GoFundMe page for her. Almost overnight, nearly a half million dollars was raised. All the people who had come and gone in her life rallied around her, advocated for her, and spread the word far and wide. It seemed as if every single person she had been kind to over the years told a few friends, who in turn told a few friends, and so on.

Even though she never expected this kind of result from her good deeds, her good karma prevailed. She was able to get the treatment she needed and survived. I wasn't surprised at all. That's how karma works!

Creating Good Karma Is Easy

Sometimes life gets crazy, and you wonder how you'll get yourself through the day, much less practice random acts of kindness. But you can be a consistent source of positive energy and good vibes if you remember these four simple techniques:

1. **Forgive.** When you hold on to a grudge, you are actually holding on to someone else's negative energy and letting it live inside of you. Instead, let it go! You do not deserve to hold on to any negative energy that was put into your life by someone else. Forgiveness does not mean you forget, however. It is a gift that you give yourself because it sets you free! When you forgive, you erase that energy from your life.

2. **Express gratitude whenever you can.** There's plenty of gratitude to go around, so be thankful for everything that's good in your life—the people who care about you, your pets, your job, the flowers in your backyard. The more conscious you are about practicing gratitude, the more good things you'll attract.

3. **Be mindful of your actions.** Have you ever been in a hurry and realized that you'd checked out of the grocery store or left the bank without thanking, or even looking at, the person who helped you? When you slow down and pay

attention, you'll find many opportunities to practice kindness with a smile, a thank-you, or a helping hand.

4. **Be kind to yourself.** How you feel inside reflects in how you treat other people, so be your own best friend! Tape positive affirmations to your bathroom mirror and avoid being overly self-critical and negative. Encourage yourself and cut yourself slack when you need it—just as you would for a loved one.

Sincere kindness, gratitude, and positivity are all simple ways to make the world a better place. Being a source of light feels good in the moment, and the good karma you earn has a way of showing up just when you need it most. I encourage you to get in the good karma habit, and practice forgiveness, gratitude, mindfulness, and acceptance every day!

Turning Bad Karma Around

I know people who did crazy and thoughtless things when they were young. Some of those people worry that those acts will catch up to them later. Karma happens, but it's not necessarily a bad thing, because it gives you a chance to handle things better the second time. There are times in life when bad karma comes back at you, but you can turn it around based on how you handle the challenge. As you grow spiritually, you become better and better at stopping the karmic cycle with awareness and consciousness.

Even if you don't feel like the universe is making you own up to your past actions, you still might feel better if you make amends. Guilt and avoidance can make you feel stuck and give you a nagging feeling that there's unfinished business you need to take care of. That's why in AA making amends is one of the steps—but you can benefit from looking back and admitting (even just to yourself) that you were wrong.

I KEEP HEARING ABOUT MERCURY RETROGRADE. WHAT IS THAT?

Have you had those moments in life where nothing goes right? Your car breaks down, deals fall through, and your computer is acting up. Chances are it's not you—it's Mercury retrograde.

Mercury is the planet of communication, and all kinds of communication gets garbled up when it's in retrograde. But what is *retrograde* and what does it have to do with the planet Mercury?

The word *retrograde* means to move backward, but when Mercury is in retrograde, the planet doesn't actually move backward, although if you were looking through a telescope, it might appear that way. It's like when you are on a train that's alongside another train in the station. When your train pulls forward, if the other train doesn't move, it feels like the other train is actually going backward.

So the feeling that Mercury is moving backward is an illusion, but its impact can feel very real! The turbulence and disruption Mercury creates when it retrogrades can affect what we feel on earth in our everyday lives.

People have different degrees of sensitivity to this energetic shift. Of course, some people don't give it a minute's thought, but there are others who alter their behavior during these times.

Some people won't sign any kind of contract when Mercury is in retrograde. I don't take it that far, but if I do sign a contract or make a major transaction, I'm extra careful, and I'm never surprised if something goes wrong!

Be Prepared to Navigate Mercury in Retrograde

My advice is to be aware, but beyond that, don't let Mercury retrograde scare you. Mark it in your calendar so you know what to expect. That way, if you need to take a flight, you can pack extra snacks for the inevitable delays!

Here's an example of what I mean. I was recording a course, and we were on a tight production schedule. I couldn't cancel filming, but I was nervous because Mercury was in retrograde.

I told the crew to be extra careful and back everything up. They were not believers, and they might have thought I was nuts, but they went along with it.

I have to admit, I was a little bit of a maniac—checking mics and cameras and reminding the crew over and over to back everything up.

After filming was over, I didn't hear from anyone for two weeks. When I called the film crew to check in, they were embarrassed. It turns out, their computer had crashed halfway through the editing process. Luckily, they had backups (thanks to me!), but they had to start editing all over again. It could have been a lot worse!

Mercury retrograde isn't something to be afraid of . . . it won't ruin your life, but it can definitely put a damper on your day. But like most things, if you're aware and prepared, you can mitigate any damage it might cause.

GOING DEEPER
Letting Go of Bad Energy

So much of the negative energy that is in your life doesn't have to be there. Here are some tips to help you avoid negative energy and keep it from "sticking" to you.

- LET IT OUT. My mom used to say that if I told her about a bad dream I had, I'd never have that same dream again. I think it works the same with the "nightmares" we experience when we're awake. I believe you shouldn't push bad feelings down. When you hang on to old traumatic experiences and don't talk about them, they have a way of staying with you and magnifying. You have to let it out. Talking about it with someone like a therapist or a friend prevents that toxic memory from having power over you.

- LET IT GO. Forgive and move on. Remember, forgiveness is a gift you give yourself—so don't feel like when you forgive someone, you're letting them off the hook. You have a choice of who you let into your life. If someone treats you badly, forgiving them doesn't mean you have to spend time with them. That's your choice. Forgiving them actually releases the energetic hold they have on you.

- JUST SAY NO. Recognize toxic people and avoid them. Your intuition and your own emotions will signal you when there's a relationship in your life that isn't serving you. Do you feel sad, unsettled, or even physically sick when you spend time with a particular person? If it happens more than once or twice, trust your gut and minimize or eliminate the time you spend with them.

You have all the power you need to protect yourself from energy vampires, old trauma, grudges, and all kinds of negative patterns. You deserve to spend your time on people and activities that bring out the best in you. Short-term it might be easier to ignore bad behavior, push down bad feelings, or tolerate an energy vampire—but in the long run, you'll be better off facing your demons and taking a stand.

One Final Question: *What do my loved ones want me to know?*

I believe being able to communicate with souls on the other side has given me a clear understanding about what's really important. When people cross over, they have the opportunity to relive their entire lives in a flash. They see the impact they had on other people, opportunities they missed, the good, the bad—everything. By talking to them, I've learned so much! It's almost as if I've been given a cheat sheet for living my best life on earth.

I know they'd want me to share what I've learned with you.

LIVING IN THE FLOW . . .

There's something in the universe called *divine flow*. What is it? It's a little like manifesting with a little boost—because you're co-creating your best life, with help from your loved ones in spirit. Let me explain. . . .

Heaven will help you when it can. Your angels will lead you to people, places, and opportunities, but they aren't going to help you cheat.

Even though I'm a psychic medium, my angels have never given me the answers to my high school math test or the lottery numbers, nor would I expect them to or ever ask them to. We are all here to live life lessons.

Learning to align with heaven through thoughts, actions, intentions, and positive expectations creates a natural flow to transform your life. I call this *divine flow*.

Something I often tell people that is a *big* surprise to them: your loved ones on the other side are creating and living the lives they wished they could have lived here. They do inspirational work; creative, incredible things that are unimaginably magnificent.

The difference is that in heaven, they have no fears or doubts or limitations. They are in divine flow. Here on earth, we are trying to come as close to that as possible, but it's difficult. There are so many physical worries and obstacles that block us from pursuing our true passions and purpose.

We all have the ability to create the lives we wish; whether we live in heaven or on earth, it is our birthright. Imagine being born with a road map in your hands. Well, you do have one. That's divine flow!

Let's do a divine flow exercise.

When You Think About the Future, How Do You Imagine It?

Would you want to get married or remarried?

Is there a divorce that has kept you stuck in limbo?

Do you want to change your career or start a business?

Do you imagine the entire life you want?

Do you want to improve your health and/or get your weight back on track?

Now that you've thought about how you'd like your future to be, here's how to use divine flow to make your dreams come true:

Act Like It Has Already Happened

Before going to bed, make your wish your mantra. For example, if you're trying to attract a romantic relationship, focus on the word *romance* or how you want to feel in that relationship. Do it for about five minutes before you go to sleep. Just see it in your mind. When we program our subconscious, the signal to the spirit world becomes strong and clear, even if we aren't fully aware of it. Focusing your intention before bed helps your subconscious and soul do the inner work while you sleep, bringing your fruitions closer when you are awake.

Ask Your Ancestors/Loved Ones for Help

Such a common ancient practice all over the world. Asking ancestors, angels, and loved ones for help with healing, protection, and comfort. And guess what? It isn't as difficult as you think. They are quite literally a part of you, which makes it easy to tap into the divine flow energy they have access to.

Gratitude Is Everything.

Think of gratitude as a cosmic savings account. Every thank-you statement you make and feel in your heart is put into this account to infuse power into your manifestations.

Unstoppable YOU

Heaven responds to our positive thoughts and feelings. When we are vibrating in a positive place, we are aligned with divine flow and our vibration is raised high enough to connect to the powerful energy of the creation. When we are in this space, we are in alignment with the flow of the universe and we feel unstoppable.

Take Inspired Action

Trust that the hunches you are receiving, such as a voice in your mind telling you to contact someone or to read a certain book or to travel somewhere, are spirits responding to your request from heaven. We are always being steered by our loved ones, angels, and spirit guides to follow the direction of our soul's passion and purpose.

Believe in the Power of the Written Word and Images

Buy a dedicated creation journal that clearly states in writing what it is you want to create. Add images! For example, the perfect car, house, and body, or a feeling . . . be very specific. Heaven will only respond to what you desire. Once you are clear and specific, write your wish in the present tense as if it is already happening. Let your imagination go wild with details. Do this for at least twenty-one days and watch the magic unfold,

People often call me an old soul, and I'm pretty sure I know why. Imagine being able to connect with souls on the other side and learn from their experiences at an early age.

You might be surprised. I don't think of myself as a spiritual teacher, but when you spend years hearing messages from heaven, like I do, you start to notice some patterns.

When you talk to heaven, they will tell you there are many different kinds of love that all contribute to your growth, development, and happiness.

I used to wonder why the souls who came through to me never seemed to hold a grudge toward anyone—even if that person had been responsible for their death. They had no guilt; they had so much confidence; they loved themselves fully . . . even after hearing that in life, they were often in pain.

Also, they didn't seem bothered if their loved one was with another person, as long as they were happy. They also all insisted on expressing love freely, stating that in life, they were not able to.

Now I realize it's because they live in heaven, but you don't have to wait until you pass over. You can experience heaven on earth! Here's how:

Taking Care of Yourself with Love, Compassion, and Forgiveness

Take a moment and listen to the way you speak to yourself, the way you feed yourself, how you keep your living space, and your sleep habits. Which of your habits and behaviors would you not allow people you love to do to themselves?

• Speaking condescendingly or down to yourself

• Leaving the television on while you sleep

• Thinking mean thoughts about yourself or others

- Eating candy before, or instead of, healthy food

- Staying up late when you're tired

- Eating while standing up, out of the package, staring at a computer screen, or watching TV

We are all guilty of these habits once in a while. But when you do them consistently, you'll probably notice that these behaviors and habits take you away from getting the things you deeply desire, like having a body you love, a job that fulfills you, a great relationship, and even having the spiritual discipline to put into practice all that you have learned in this book.

Put Self-Parenting on Top of Your List

Look back at your relationship with your parents and/or your children and identify the parenting techniques that worked the best for you. I'll bet it was a mix of being strong and consistent in enforcing the rules, while also being kind, patient, and understanding. Create a list of rules and promises. If you're new to this, keep the list small, then keep adding to it and you will see success. Keep it manageable. Looking back at my childhood, there were a lot of things that were nonnegotiable that ultimately created great habits.

Align Yourself with Your Purpose

Remember, finding your purpose is about learning how to use your divine gifts. On page 174 I go over this process—see the section Why Am I Here? How Can I Discover My True Purpose?

Find Your Unique Talent or Gift

If you can't readily identify what makes you unique, look at what you love. What conversations or activities excite you most? What are you better at than anyone else you know? When we work in these places of our brilliance, time disappears as we become completely one with the creation. Think about the struggles and challenges that you have gone through in your life. How could you use those skills to help someone going through the same or something similar?

WHY WE NEVER DIE

If there is one thing that your loved ones in spirit want for you to know, it's that the more you learn about heaven and the afterlife, the more you will learn that it is not a faraway place and, more important, there is no such thing as death—it's just a change of worlds.

As painful as it is to lose a loved one, they still remain with you here on earth. They watch over you, guide you, and most important, they still love you with all of their heart and soul. The signs of their spiritual presence are all around you and appear in many different forms, and the ways in which they communicate with you are endless.

But there is a secret, and it's the reason why I decided to write this book. You can also communicate back and stay connected with your loved ones on a daily basis. It starts with recognizing and sensing their spiritual presence in your life and knowing that they will receive the message.

Remember that love is a divine glue. It's a deep connection that keeps us connected to those we love even when they leave this world. The best part about this connection is that it cannot be destroyed; it only grows stronger over time.

Always remember that conversation is a two-way street. As much as you love hearing from your loved ones in spirit, they also love hearing from you.

When you think about them, speak to them or reminisce about the times you had with them. It's like ringing the doorbell to heaven and saying hello.

You can communicate with them at any time. No matter where you are or what you are doing, they will hear you.

How is that possible you ask? The answer is simple: We never die.

· ACKNOWLEDGMENTS ·

I cannot believe this is my second published book with Simon & Schuster and Gallery Books. I literally have chills right now writing this. This would not have been possible without the amazing team that stood with me to make this happen. So here is a big thank-you from me to you.

Alexa, my wife: Thank you for the beautiful foreword, and for the love and joy that you have brought into my life. I love having you here on this journey with me.

Thank you to my mom, Angela, my dad, Roderick, and my sister, Maria, for their constant love and reassurance.

To Imal Wagner, my longtime publicist: Can you believe we started this back in 2011!? Now here we are, three published books later, with a reality TV series and national news appearances under our belts, all because of you and your constant faith in me. Everything in my life and career is because of you. I don't know how to thank you.

To Lisa Marie Tucker, my executive producer and friend: I thank you for always lifting me up and for your constant faith and belief in me.

To Ricardo Couto, my current tour manager: Thank you so much for literally running all over the country with me on tour. Thank you for being a problem solver and babysitter, and for all the laughs we have had together on this incredible journey.

To Seth Shomes, my tour agent: Thank you for bringing me to so many amazing cities and venues. I always enjoy our calls together and your amazing sense of humor. You are always lifting me up.

To Dominic Joseph, my production assistant and now tour producer: Thank you for making each show so spectacular.

To Sherry Ferdinandi, my CFO and business manager: Thank you for handling everything! Because of you I can focus on my life's work and mission and not have to worry about the day-to-day business. Thank you for constantly fighting for me and for my best interests.

To Alice and Patrick, my marketing directors: Thank you for taking my thoughts and visions and transforming them into art!

To my editor, Jeremie Ruby-Strauss: I cannot believe we are on our second book together! This book is one that I have wanted to write for so long! Thank you for believing in me and making this dream become a reality. It is because of you that I've been able to have my books published with Simon & Schuster and I will always be grateful to you for this amazing opportunity. I owe you everything.

Molly Gregory, thank you so much for managing calls, coordinating teams, and keeping everyone in constant communication. Everything you did made this all happen so quickly.

Caroline Pallotta, thank you so much for keeping me on track with the timeline of this book! Even though a lot of your work was behind the scenes, I know how hard you worked to make sure that everything was completed on time. It means the world to me.

Sarah Wright, thank God I had you to proofread and correct all of my many mistakes. I have no idea how I passed English! Because of you, nobody will ever know just how bad my grammar, spelling, and punctuation actually are! Hopefully we can keep this secret to ourselves.

Jennifer Robinson, I will always think back to our time together on our press tour in New York City and our many conversations on the tour stops. From being on air with Jenny McCarthy to frantically getting copies of the book to give to audience members on *The Doctors* BEFORE it was printed, you are an MVP and I am so thankful for how hard you work. Thank you for being my literary publicist.

Mackenzie Hickey, my marketing specialist: Thank you for making sure that my books make it onto the shelves of all the bookstores! When I walk by the bookstores and see my book in the window, I always think of you.

John Vairo and Lisa Litwack, my creative art directors: I cannot begin to tell you how obsessed I am with this book cover! It is so beautiful, different, and unique. John, I love your can-do attitude and your vision! You are a creative genius!

Jen Bergstrom, thank you for helping me to get this book into the hands of grieving people around the world. These messages are so important and I know that this book will help so many who are grieving the loss of a loved one. I am so thankful to have you as my publisher.

Aimee Bell, thank you for sharing in this vision of my book and for all your help behind the scenes. I cannot wait for people to start reading what we worked on.

Jen Long, I will never forget meeting you at the Simon & Schuster headquarters in NYC and how genuinely excited you were to start this project. Thank you for all the delicious snacks, coffee, and hallway conversations. So excited to continue working with you as deputy publisher.

Sally Marvin, thank you for all of your help with getting the word out! I am so thankful to have you as my publicity and marketing director for this book.

To all my friends, family, and the entire team at Simon & Schuster: I am truly thankful to all of you. I count my blessings every day for having you all.